HERNÁN
CORTÉS

HERNÁN CORTÉS

Dennis Wepman

1986
CHELSEA HOUSE PUBLISHERS
NEW YORK
NEW HAVEN   PHILADELPHIA

SENIOR EDITOR: William P. Hansen
PROJECT EDITOR: John W. Selfridge
ASSOCIATE EDITOR: Marian W. Taylor
EDITORIAL COORDINATOR: Karyn Gullen Browne
EDITORIAL STAFF: Maria Behan
        Pierre Hauser
        Perry Scott King
        Kathleen McDermott
        Howard Ratner
        Alma Rodriguez-Sokol
        Bert Yaeger
ART DIRECTOR: Susan Lusk
LAYOUT: Irene Friedman
ART ASSISTANTS: Noreen Lamb
        Carol McDougall
        Victoria Tomaselli
COVER ILLUSTRATION: Richard Leonard
PICTURE RESEARCH: Ian Ensign

Frontispiece courtesy of The Bettmann Archive

First Printing

Library of Congress Cataloging in Publication Data

Wepman, Dennis. HERNÁN CORTÉS

(World leaders past & present)
Bibliography: p.
Includes index.
  1. Cortés, Hernán, 1485–1547.   2. Explorers—Mexico—Biography.
3. Explorers—Spain—Biography. [1. Cortés, Hernando, 1485–1547.
2. Explorers]   I. Title.   II. Series.
F1230.C835W46   1986   972'.01'0924 [B] [92]   85-6719

ISBN 0-87754-593-6

Chelsea House Publishers
Harold Steinberg, Chairman and Publisher
Susan Lusk, Vice President
A Division of Chelsea House Educational Communications, Inc.

133 Christopher Street, New York, NY 10014

345 Whitney Avenue, New Haven, CT 06510

5014 West Chester Pike, Edgemont, PA 19028

Contents

CHELSEA HOUSE PUBLISHERS

WORLD LEADERS PAST & PRESENT

ADENAUER
ALEXANDER THE GREAT
MARK ANTONY
KING ARTHUR
KEMAL ATATÜRK
CLEMENT ATTLEE
BEGIN
BEN-GURION
BISMARCK
LEON BLUM
BOLÍVAR
CESARE BORGIA
BRANDT
BREZHNEV
CAESAR
CALVIN
CASTRO
CATHERINE THE GREAT
CHARLEMAGNE
CHIANG KAI-SHEK
CHURCHILL
CLEMENCEAU
CLEOPATRA
CORTÉS
CROMWELL
DANTON
DE GAULLE
DE VALERA
DISRAELI
EISENHOWER
ELEANOR OF AQUITAINE
QUEEN ELIZABETH I
FERDINAND AND ISABELLA

FRANCO
FREDERICK THE GREAT
INDIRA GANDHI
GANDHI
GARIBALDI
GENGHIS KHAN
GLADSTONE
HAMMARSKJÖLD
HENRY VIII
HENRY OF NAVARRE
HINDENBURG
HITLER
HO CHI MINH
KING HUSSEIN
IVAN THE TERRIBLE
ANDREW JACKSON
JEFFERSON
JOAN OF ARC
POPE JOHN XXIII
LYNDON JOHNSON
BENITO JUÁREZ
JFK
KENYATTA
KHOMEINI
KHRUSHCHEV
MARTIN LUTHER KING, JR.
KISSINGER
LENIN
LINCOLN
LLOYD GEORGE
LOUIS XIV
LUTHER
JUDAS MACCABEUS
MAO

MARY, QUEEN OF SCOTS
GOLDA MEIR
METTERNICH
MUSSOLINI
NAPOLEON
NASSER
NEHRU
NERO
NICHOLAS II
NIXON
NKRUMAH
PERICLES
PERÓN
QADDAFI
ROBESPIERRE
ELEANOR ROOSEVELT
FDR
THEODORE ROOSEVELT
SADAT
STALIN
SUN YAT-SEN
TAMERLAINE
THATCHER
TITO
TROTSKY
TRUDEAU
TRUMAN
QUEEN VICTORIA
WASHINGTON
CHAIM WEIZMANN
WOODROW WILSON
XERXES
ZHOU ENLAI

ON LEADERSHIP
Arthur M. Schlesinger, jr.

LEADERSHIP, it may be said, is really what makes the world go round. Love no doubt smooths the passage; but love is a private transaction between consenting adults. Leadership is a public transaction with history. The idea of leadership affirms the capacity of individuals to move, inspire and mobilize masses of people so that they act together in pursuit of an end. Sometimes leadership serves good purposes, sometimes bad; but whether the end is benign or evil, great leaders are those men and women who leave their personal stamp on history.

Now, the very concept of leadership implies the proposition that individuals can make a difference. This proposition has never been universally accepted. From classical times to the present day, eminent thinkers have regarded individuals as no more than the agents and pawns of larger forces, whether the gods and goddesses of the ancient world or, in the modern era, race, class, nation, the dialectic, the will of the people, the spirit of the times, history itself. Against such forces, the individual dwindles into insignificance.

So contends the thesis of historical determinism. Tolstoy's great novel *War and Peace* offers a famous statement of the case. Why, Tolstoy asked, did millions of men in the Napoleonic wars, denying their human feelings and their common sense, move back and forth across Europe slaughtering their fellows? "The war," Tolstoy answered, "was bound to happen simply because it was bound to happen." All prior history predetermined it. As for leaders, they, Tolstoy said, "are but the labels that serve to give a name to an end and, like labels, they have the least possible connection with the event." The greater the leader, "the more conspicuous the inevitability and the predestination of every act he commits." The leader, said Tolstoy, is "the slave of history."

Determinism takes many forms. Marxism is the determinism of class, Nazism the determinism of race. But the idea of men and women as the slaves of history runs athwart the deepest human instincts. Rigid determinism abolishes the idea of human freedom—the assumption of free choice that underlies every move we make, every word we speak, every thought we think. It abolishes the idea of human responsibility, since it is manifestly unfair to reward or punish people for actions that are by definition beyond their control. No one can live consistently by any deterministic creed. The Marxist states prove this themselves by their extreme susceptibility to the cult of leadership.

More than that, history refutes the idea that individuals make no difference. In December 1931 a British politician crossing Park Avenue in New York City between 76th and 77th Streets around ten-thirty at night looked in the wrong direction and was knocked down by an automobile—a moment, he later recalled, of a man aghast, a world aglare: "I do not understand why I was not broken like an eggshell or squashed like a gooseberry." Fourteen months later an American politician, sitting in an open car in Miami, Florida, was fired on by an assassin; the man beside him was hit. Those who believe that individuals make no difference to history might well ponder whether the next two decades would have been the same had Mario Contasini's car killed Winston Churchill in 1931 and Giuseppe Zangara's bullet killed Franklin Roosevelt in 1933. Suppose, in addition, that Adolf Hitler had been killed in the street fighting during the Munich *Putsch* of 1923 and that Lenin had died of typhus during the First World War. What would the 20th century be like now?

For better or for worse, individuals do make a difference. "The notion that a people can run itself and its affairs anonymously," wrote the philosopher William James, "is now well known to be the silliest of absurdities. Mankind does nothing save through initiatives on the part of inventors, great or small, and imitation by the rest of us—these are the sole factors in human progress. Individuals of genius show the way, and set the patterns, which common people then adopt and follow."

Leadership, James suggests, means leadership in thought as well as in action. In the long run, leaders in thought may well make the greater difference to the world. But, as Woodrow Wilson once said, "Those only are leaders of men, in the general eye, who lead in action. . . . It is at their hands that new thought gets its translation into the crude language of deeds." Leaders in thought often invent in solitude and obscurity, leaving to later generations the tasks of imitation. Leaders in action—the leaders portrayed in this series—have to be effective in their own time.

And they cannot be effective by themselves. They must act in response to the rhythms of their age. Their genius must be adapted, in a phrase of William James's, "to the receptivities of the moment." Leaders are useless without followers. "There goes the mob," said the French politician hearing a clamor in the streets. "I am their leader. I must follow them." Great leaders turn the inchoate emotions of the mob to purposes of their own. They seize on the opportunities of their time, the hopes, fears, frustrations, crises, potentialities.

They succeed when events have prepared the way for them, when the community is waiting to be aroused, when they can provide the clarifying and organizing ideas. Leadership ignites the circuit between the individual and the mass and thereby alters history.

It may alter history for better or for worse. Leaders have been responsible for the most extravagant follies and most monstrous crimes that have beset suffering humanity. They have also been vital in such gains as humanity has made in individual freedom, religious and racial tolerance, social justice and respect for human rights.

There is no sure way to tell in advance who is going to lead for good and who for evil. But a glance at the gallery of men and women in *World Leaders—Past and Present* suggests some useful tests.

One test is this: do leaders lead by force or by persuasion? By command or by consent? Through most of history leadership was exercised by the divine right of authority. The duty of followers was to defer and to obey. "Theirs not to reason why,/ Theirs but to do and die." On occasion, as with the so-called "enlightened despots" of the 18th century in Europe, absolutist leadership was animated by humane purposes. More often, absolutism nourished the passion for domination, land, gold and conquest and resulted in tyranny.

The great revolution of modern times has been the revolution of equality. The idea that all people should be equal in their legal condition has undermined the old structures of authority, hierarchy and deference. The revolution of equality has had two contrary effects on the nature of leadership. For equality, as Alexis de Tocqueville pointed out in his great study *Democracy in America*, might mean equality in servitude as well as equality in freedom.

"I know of only two methods of establishing equality in the political world," Tocqueville wrote. "Rights must be given to every citizen, or none at all to anyone . . . save one, who is the master of all." There was no middle ground "between the sovereignty of all and the absolute power of one man." In his astonishing prediction of 20th-century totalitarian dictatorship, Tocqueville explained how the revolution of equality could lead to the "*Führerprinzip*" and more terrible absolutism than the world had ever known.

But when rights are given to every citizen and the sovereignty of all is established, the problem of leadership takes a new form, becomes more exacting than ever before. It is easy to issue commands and enforce them by the rope and the stake, the concentration camp and the *gulag*. It is much harder to use argument and achievement to overcome opposition and win consent. The Founding Fathers of the United States understood the difficulty. They believed that history had given them the opportunity to decide, as

Alexander Hamilton wrote in the first Federalist Paper, whether men arc indeed capable of basing government on "reflection and choice, or whether they are forever destined to depend . . . on accident and force."

Government by reflection and choice called for a new style of leadership and a new quality of followership. It required leaders to be responsive to popular concerns, and it required followers to be active and informed participants in the process. Democracy does not eliminate emotion from politics; sometimes it fosters demagoguery; but it is confident that, as the greatest of democratic leaders put it, you cannot fool all of the people all of the time. It measures leadership by results and retires those who overreach or falter or fail.

It is true that in the long run despots are measured by results too. But they can postpone the day of judgment, sometimes indefinitely, and in the meantime they can do infinite harm. It is also true that democracy is no guarantee of virtue and intelligence in government, for the voice of the people is not necessarily the voice of God. But democracy, by assuring the rights of opposition, offers built-in resistance to the evils inherent in absolutism. As the theologian Reinhold Niebuhr summed it up, "Man's capacity for justice makes democracy possible, but man's inclination to injustice makes democracy necessary."

A second test for leadership is the end for which power is sought. When leaders have as their goal the supremacy of a master race or the promotion of totalitarian revolution or the acquisition and exploitation of colonies or the protection of greed and privilege or the preservation of personal power, it is likely that their leadership will do little to advance the cause of humanity. When their goal is the abolition of slavery, the liberation of women, the enlargement of opportunity for the poor and powerless, the extension of equal rights to racial minorities, the defense of the freedoms of expression and opposition, it is likely that their leadership will increase the sum of human liberty and welfare.

Leaders have done great harm to the world. They have also conferred great benefits. You will find both sorts in this series. Even "good" leaders must be regarded with a certain wariness. Leaders are not demigods; they put on their trousers one leg after another just like ordinary mortals. No leader is infallible, and every leader needs to be reminded of this at regular intervals. Irreverence irritates leaders but is their salvation. Unquestioning submission corrupts leaders and demeans followers. Making a cult of a leader is always a mistake. Fortunately hero worship generates its own antidote. "Every hero," said Emerson, "becomes a bore at last."

The signal benefit the great leaders confer is to embolden the rest of us to live according to our own best selves, to be active, insistent, and resolute in affirming our own sense of things. For great leaders attest to the reality of human freedom against the supposed inevitabilities of history. And they attest to the wisdom and power that may lie within the most unlikely of us, which is why Abraham Lincoln remains the supreme example of great leadership. A great leader, said Emerson, exhibits new possibilities to all humanity. "We feed on genius. . . . Great men exist that there may be greater men."

Great leaders, in short, justify themselves by emancipating and empowering their followers. So humanity struggles to master its destiny, remembering with Alexis de Tocqueville: "It is true that around every man a fatal circle is traced beyond which he cannot pass; but within the wide verge of that circle he is powerful and free; as it is with man, so with communities."

—*New York*

1

The Scholar

Spain was an especially exciting place at the beginning of the 16th century. The country was in its own squalling infancy, and the possibilities for wealth and power seemed boundless. The merger of the kingdoms of Castile and Aragon in 1479 had given the Catholic monarchs Ferdinand and Isabella a real country to rule, and they set about vigorously expanding and enriching it. In 1492, after nearly 800 years of Muslim rule, Spain had finally overthrown the intruders when Ferdinand's troops took Granada, the last Muslim stronghold. In a religious and patriotic frenzy, the country expelled the Jews the same year.

It was also in that year that the Spanish rulers, in their fever for expansion, financed the scheme of an Italian explorer named Christopher Columbus to find an ocean route west to Asia. He never did, of course, but he found something much better. He found a new world. And his discoveries opened the door to the most exciting period the Old World had ever known.

That fever of adventure and change was still in the air seven years later, in the last year of the century, when a young Spaniard arrived in the famous

Portrait of Hernán Cortés (1485–1547), the Spanish conqueror of Mexico. Lured by tales of adventure and the promise of gold, Cortés left Spain in 1504 at the age of 19 to seek fame and fortune in the West Indies.

ART RESOURCE

A woodcut dating from 1493 depicts the explorer Christopher Columbus (1451–1506) sailing in the West Indies. The Italian captain's expedition was financed by the Spanish rulers Ferdinand (1452–1516) and Isabella (1451–1504), who were actively seeking to expand their empire. Columbus discovered the islands while searching for an ocean route west to Asia.

The Spanish military leader Santiago, battling Muslims at Granada. The victory of the Christian forces in January 1492 was the culmination of a 10-year campaign against the last Moorish stronghold in Spain, ending eight centuries of Muslim rule on the Iberian peninsula.

old university town of Salamanca. Hernán Cortés was only 14—young even in those days to enter a university—but he was a bright, resourceful boy who had already begun to show promise. It was apparent that he had a certain talent for getting into trouble, and his religious, highly respectable family decided it was time for him to pursue a career. Hernán agreed with them and, with relief, shook off the dust of his little provincial town of Medellín. It was in Estremadura, one of the poorest and bleakest provinces in Spain, and he saw little future for himself there.

There were only three choices of career open to a Spanish gentleman in those days: the Church, the army, or the law. Physical work was felt to be beneath the dignity of a man of pure blood, and business was almost as great a disgrace. But a good scholar could hope to gain a powerful position within the hierarchy of the Roman Catholic church or to become a magistrate. And there was almost no limit to what a soldier could become.

Hernán was clearly unsuited to the priesthood. His sickliness as a child would preclude him from entering the army. But since he was, according to his first biographer, Francisco López de Gómara, "restless, haughty, mischievous, and given to quarreling," a career as a lawyer seemed appropriate. The spirited youth saw himself a powerful magistrate, presiding over great courts.

In 1499 Hernán was a little too easily distracted to be a really serious student, though there is evidence that he learned a great deal in his two years at the University of Salamanca. There are no records of his schoolwork, and later reports do not always agree. One biographer maintains he left school because of illness, another because of lack of funds. Most of those who knew him later, however, thought that boredom was the main reason he returned home at age 16.

Hernán's time at the university had been well spent. Young Cortés had unwittingly made important preparations for the future. For Cortés would one day conquer and administer a great empire. In so doing he would have much need of all the knowledge of law and government that he had gained at Salamanca.

When Cortés returned to Medellín, his family was none too pleased to see him. It was an old, distinguished family with "little wealth but much honor," as one chronicler put it. Cortés's parents had set their hopes on their only child, and the restless boy seemed likely to be a disappointment to them. The naturally hot-blooded Cortés felt stifled by the conventions of his provincial hometown.

Although Cortés's failure to win a university degree did not rule out a career in the Church, his sexual appetites did. He had long since outgrown the frailty of his childhood, which, according to one account, was so great that "many times he was on the point of dying." The two aimless and idle years that Cortés spent at home after he quit school accomplished little besides the torment of his parents. By the time he was 18, he would have done anything to get out of the house—anything, that is, except return to school. What Cortés wanted was action, and neither the law court nor the altar could ever provide that. Perhaps the answer was the army or—a new possibility—adventure in the Indies.

Columbus's fantastic stories were still much in the news in Spain. The fabulous new lands he had discovered were still imperfectly understood, and, for that reason, were all the more thrilling to contemplate. Indians and golden trinkets from the New World had already made their appearance in the cities. Sailors were showing off the use of tobacco and terrifying the ladies by blowing smoke out of their mouths. Brilliant-colored parrots were screeching and droll monkeys cavorting in the streets. What high-spirited boy of 18 would not have felt drawn to the prospects of adventure, fame, and gold?

An amorous escapade cost Cortés his first opportunity to travel to the Indies (as the islands discovered by Columbus were known). His father's old commanding officer in the army, Nicolás de Ovando, had been appointed governor-general of the Indies and had agreed to take young Cortés with him. Shortly before Ovando's scheduled departure,

Whether he was a bachelor of law or not, we can see [that Cortés possessed] a masterly hand with men, a masterly mind with things, a gift for expression.
—SALVADOR DE MADARIAGA
Cortés biographer

Cortés was nearly killed escaping from the house of a married woman when her husband discovered him. Only the intervention of the wife's mother kept him from being spitted on the husband's sword. As it was, he was injured slightly when a wall he was climbing during his escape collapsed. By the time Cortés recovered, Ovando had left.

It must have been frustrating to come this close to a great adventure and lose the chance, and the boy was now undecided as to his future. He thought seriously of joining the army—a more respectable career for a Spanish gentleman of good family than that of a soldier of fortune anyway. The Spanish were fighting in Italy under Gonzalo Fernández de Córdoba, a brilliant soldier who was known as "the Great Captain."

A map illustrating the partitioning of Spain into several distinct regions, later known as fiefdoms. This pattern persisted until 1479, when Isabella of Castile and Ferdinand II of Aragon married, merging Spain's two largest kingdoms. Isabella's husband took the name Ferdinand V of Castile.

17

Columbus at the court of Ferdinand and Isabella. News of Columbus's journeys spread quickly throughout Spain and fired the imagination of the young Cortés. He had been less than enthusiastic about a career as a priest or magistrate, the occupations expected of a man from a respectable family.

Cortés never quite committed himself to soldiering in Italy. He went to Valencia, the first step on the way to Italy, but was sidetracked. Soon he was traveling around without money or destination, picking up a meal and a bed when he could find them. He wandered around Spain for about a year before he tired of it and returned home.

Cortés was now almost 20 years old. His family had been very indulgent. They had supported him in school for two years even though it had obviously bored him. They had tolerated three subsequent years of indecision and carousing. But even their patience had limits. They reached into their pockets once more and packed him off to the New World.

Cortés's parents probably did not regard this as an investment in the future. Perhaps they were indulging his love of adventure again, or making a display of their own patriotism by sending their only son to serve Spain in its new territories. Not the least of their reasons was probably a desperate desire to get their son gainfully employed at something and off their hands. Whatever prompted their decision, the family got its money's worth. They set in motion a train of events that was to alter the course of history and make the name Cortés immortal.

A 16th-century engraving depicting Columbus's first landing in the New World. Columbus believed he had reached Asia, and thus called the natives Indians. Actually, he probably landed on an island in the Bahamas, halfway around the globe from India.

BERTRAND.

2

The Adventurer

I came to get gold, not to till the soil like a peasant.
—HERNÁN CORTÉS
Hispaniola, 1504

In 1504 Cortés set sail from the port of Seville, where most of the gold of the Indies first arrived in Spain. Everywhere around him he saw tantalizing evidence of the riches of the New World, but he took passage for Hispaniola with no real idea of what lay before him.

Hispaniola (now Haiti and the Dominican Republic) was the capital of the Indies, and young men went there to find their fortunes or make names for themselves. Some went to serve God and bring the Christian faith to the native population. Others went for fame and even aspired to found cities. Almost all went for gold. Social advancement was difficult for even the most ambitious in the old, established aristocracy of Spain, but Hispaniola was wide-open—a new frontier. The rugged, the cunning, and the desperate of Spain sailed into the Indies at the beginning of the 16th century just as Americans were to travel to California in quest of gold three centuries later.

Cortés took passage on one of five ships carrying supplies to Santo Domingo, the capital of Hispaniola. Shortly after a stopover in the Canary Islands, his ship ran into a storm that snapped off its mast

Hernán Cortés in a suit of armor, around 1505. Cortés's early participation in military expeditions on the island of Hispaniola whetted his appetite for further exploration and conquest.

THE NEW YORK PUBLIC LIBRARY

Cortés, one of many young men seeking a future in the New World, bids adieu to his native land in 1504 as his ship leaves the port of Seville.

Four Portuguese explorers, including Vasco da Gama (1460–1524), at upper right. In the late 1490s da Gama discovered a sea route to India from Europe by navigating around the Cape of Good Hope, the southern tip of Africa. At the time, Spain and Portugal were racing to "open up" Asia for trade and commercial exploitation.

and sent it limping back to port almost as soon as it set sail.

Cortés did not allow this setback to dampen his enthusiasm. After hasty repairs, the ship again set sail. This time the vessel got lost when high winds blew it off course. Everyone feared for his life. They all said confession and resigned themselves to dying of thirst or being shipwrecked on the cannibal islands of the Caribbean.

But on Good Friday a white dove touched down on the ship—a traditional sign of divine protection—and, as the story goes, everyone knew he was saved. In fact, within hours they spotted Hispaniola. "Weeping with joy," according to one account, the passengers and crew sailed safely into harbor.

Cortés went straight from the ship to Governor-General Ovando, confident that this old friend of his father's would immediately set him on the road to easy riches. He was in for his first disappointment. Cortés was not the first adventurer to learn with dismay that there was little gold on the island. Lush and fertile, it could make a man rich—but only if he worked hard at farming it.

But no one had come from Spain to toil on the land. In fact, Columbus, "the Discoverer," had set up a system of forced labor in which natives were distributed to the settlers as slaves, to farm the land for them, look for gold, and serve in their homes. The native tribes of Hispaniola did not always accept this slavery passively, and there were frequent small rebellions. This tended to make life both unpleasant and dangerous for the settlers. As a last resort, Columbus had been forced to order the Spanish to do some of the work themselves. Many objected, and reports of his mistreatment of the Spanish and his cruelty to the natives reached the king, who promptly had Columbus sent home in chains.

Columbus had later been pardoned, given a few more grand titles, and sent off on another expedition with strict orders to stay out of Hispaniola. It would take the diplomatic efforts of Ovando to establish peace and stability on the island.

Ovando made a standard offer to any Spaniard looking for a home on the island. He would give him

An Arabic conception of the monsters that haunted the sea. Tales about supernatural ocean creatures were part of Spain's Moorish legacy taken to heart by Spanish sailors of Cortés's day.

a farm lot and a team of natives to work it. After five years, if the settler proved diligent and productive, the land was his. Because Cortés had had two years of college and was, more importantly, the son of an army officer, Ovando offered him, in addition to the farm and laborers, the post of notary in the settlement of Azúa, 50 hard miles from Santo Domingo. Although Cortés did not believe Ovando's warning that he would do better as a farmer than as an adventurer, he curbed his impatience—at least for the time being. He dutifully farmed his land, and also made a little extra money as a notary, but this life was hardly more exciting than the one he had left behind in Estremadura. As for the hope of gold, the little gold dust that his natives were able to turn up was hardly worth his time to measure. Despite these disappointments, life in Azúa did have its amusements. There was gambling and drinking with his fellow planters, and there were always romantic involvements to keep life from becoming too dull.

During this period, Cortés got to practice the fighting skills that would prove useful later. Ovando was constantly beleaguered by native uprisings and sent his lieutenant, Diego Velásquez, to suppress them. When Cortés was not out hunting wild pigs or chasing native women, he "found means," as the American historian William H. Prescott writes, "of breaking up the monotony" by joining Velásquez's expeditions. Thus, Cortés became acquainted with

Map of the West Indies. European colonial powers, led by the Spanish but followed in time by the English, French, and Dutch, carved out spheres of influence on these lush and fertile islands.

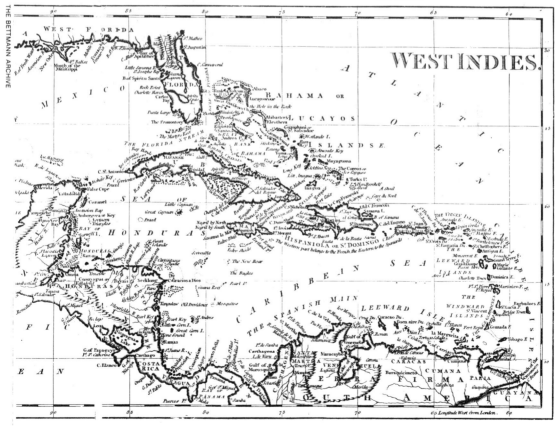

danger and the "wild tactics" of native warfare.

Cortés undoubtedly enjoyed the free life, without any of the restrictions of Spanish law and his religious home, but he had already had a taste of that freedom in Spain. However, he was seeking fame and fortune, and the life of a provincial farmer was earning him neither. There is even a story that he had to share his one good cape with two other men, who took turns wearing it when they went out in public.

To Cortés, participating in Velásquez's campaigns against the Taino Indians now began to seem vastly preferable to stagnating indefinitely in Azúa. Velásquez was an important man, the governor of the province, answering only to the governor-general, Ovando.

Velásquez, one of the earliest settlers in the Indies, had founded four thriving towns and now held more land than any other man on the island. A Spanish chronicler described his disposition as "attractive and merry," and said that while he liked to give the impression of being slow-witted, he was actually one of the most ruthless, clever, and greedy men in the New World. Most people who came into conflict with him lived to regret it, though often not for long. Cortés noted the relentlessness with which Velásquez slaughtered whole tribes of Indians—hostile and friendly alike—and made a profit from every expedition. The young adventurer soon decided that Velásquez might be a useful man to know.

After five years in the New World, Cortés had grown impatient with Hispaniola and the life of a farmer. But there were prospects. The Spanish empire was slowly expanding. Ovando sent out ships to explore and claim more land for the greater glory of God and the greater riches of the Spanish.

Columbus had fought for his rights to the country he had discovered ever since he was sent home in disgrace. In 1506 the Discoverer died, still protesting. His son, Diego Colón (the family had by now adopted the Spanish form of the name), inherited his father's impressive title of viceroy of the Indies, but little else. Colón determined to make the title worth something, and finally got himself appointed

> *We Spanish suffer from a disease of the heart which can be cured only by gold.*
> —HERNÁN CORTÉS

THE BETTMANN ARCHIVE

as Ovando's replacement in 1509. If the father could find the lands, he reasoned, the son could make them pay.

Colón sent a fleet to take over Puerto Rico almost immediately, and had little trouble conquering its native population. However, the Puerto Rican Indians were too savage to be easily enslaved, and the land turned out to be good for nothing but agriculture. The Spanish were looking for quick returns on their investment and turned hopefully to Jamaica. This small island, though pretty and fertile, did not prove any richer in gold than Puerto Rico.

Columbus died without ever understanding what he had discovered, and to the end insisted that Cuba was part of the mainland of Asia. By now, everyone knew it was an island, though no one was

Columbus in chains, 1495–96. Columbus's brutal treatment of natives and settlers alike brought on rebellion and ultimately Columbus's arrest by Spanish authorities. He was later pardoned by the king, but the conflicts in the New World had only just begun.

certain whether it was the fabled isle of gold or just another big tract of farmland. The enterprising Colón was willing to invest some money and men to find out.

Since its discovery by Columbus, the Spanish had done some superficial exploring on Cuba, then called Fernandina in honor of King Ferdinand. It was known to have rich soil and a friendly Indian population that lacked the means to resist colonization and enslavement. Gold or no gold, the island seemed worth taking. It could be used as land for future Spanish settlers and as a source of Indian labor. In 1511 Colón called on Velásquez to lead an expedition of conquest to Cuba.

Velásquez was getting old and had become fat, but he was still, according to a contemporary, "covetous of glory, and somewhat more covetous of wealth." He outfitted four ships and recruited 300 adventurers to take over the giant island.

Cortés was 26 by now. Utterly disenchanted with farm life, and still craving action, he viewed the expedition to Cuba with great interest. His college training and experience as a notary won him the

This map of the world was made by German navigator and geographer Martin Behaim (1436–1507) in 1492, before Columbus's discoveries. Note the absence of any reference on the map to the Americas.

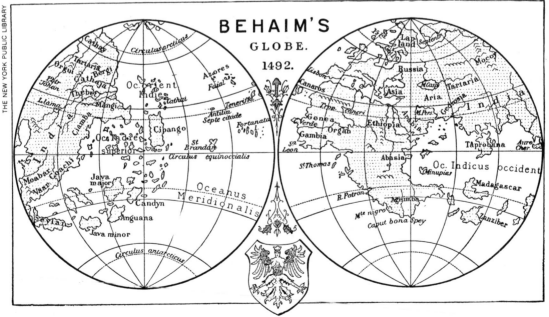

Indians resisting a Spanish expedition. Efforts by explorers to expand Spanish holdings in the West Indies often involved bloody battles with the natives. The Spanish usually prevailed since the Indians' bows and arrows proved useless against the superior power of Spanish firearms.

job of secretary to Velásquez, and since Velásquez was past his prime as a fighter, Cortés became his right-hand man in the field as well as his chief military adviser. In a short time, he became more influential with Velásquez than anyone else on the expedition except, perhaps, Pánfilo de Narváez, Velásquez's second-in-command.

The good-looking and friendly young Cortés soon made himself popular with the troops. They were all there for the same thing, and excitement and fellowship ran high among them. The aristocratic Cortés had a natural charm that greatly enhanced his authority; by the end of 1511, he and his troops were functioning as a well-organized unit, and were on their way to creating an empire.

3

The Settler

Conquering new territories was no easy task. In 1509 two Spanish adventurers, made confident by the quick submission of Puerto Rico and Jamaica, had set off for Panama with 1,000 men. They had been wiped out by fierce Indians and by the treachery of those among their compatriots whose greed exceeded their own. Cortés had tried to join that expedition, too. It is another example of his rare good luck that he was recovering from an illness when the expedition sailed, so he missed the boat again, but reports of the disaster did not discourage him from trying again two years later.

In 1511 an expedition organized and supported by Colón arrived in Cuba. The Indians of Cuba, related to those of Hispaniola, were docile and submissive, and Narváez, who undertook to clear the forests of them, encountered only sparse resistance. The Spanish dealt brutally with the few natives who fought back, meting out cruel punishments to keep the rest of the island's population in line. When Hatuey, a native of Hispaniola who had fled to Cuba to escape Velásquez's massacre, was captured, he was sentenced to be burned alive. As they tied him to the stake, the priests offered him a chance to convert to Christianity to ensure that his soul would go to heaven. But when Hatuey learned that white men went to heaven, he refused the offer.

Hernán Cortés, around 1511. During that year he served under Diego Velásquez (1465–1524) in the Spanish conquest of Cuba. In this new colony, Cortés became a rich plantation owner and an important official.

THE NEW YORK PUBLIC LIBRARY

Cortés asking Governor Velásquez for a pardon, 1515. Concerned about Cortés's rising power, Velásquez tried at first to ruin Cortés by bringing charges against him. The governor subsequently granted Cortés a pardon in order to enlist his aid in suppressing an Indian uprising.

Nicolaus Copernicus (1473–1543), Polish astronomer who theorized that the sun—not the earth—was the center of the planetary system. Scientific discoveries, as well as those made by seafaring explorers of the 14th and 15th centuries, altered man's perception of his place on earth.

Velásquez was made governor of Cuba, and began to develop it as efficiently as Ovando had developed Hispaniola. He founded several cities, developed the sugar-cane industry, opened gold mines, and lured settlers from Spain with grants of land and slaves. The first big land grant he issued was to his favorite, Hernán Cortés.

Cortés had proved a brave, loyal, skillful soldier and had built a considerable following among the army of the new colony. Velásquez considered Cortés a valuable ally, and eagerly supported him in his enterprises. Cortés built the first house in the capital, Santiago, and raised the first cattle and sheep. He became the mayor of the first city of Cuba. With the help of his Indians, he found gold and soon made himself one of the richest, most prominent citizens of the island.

An early map of Brazil, showing Cabo de San Augustin, the first Spanish settlement in South America. Spanish colonial efforts were not limited to the West Indies—explorers and settlers also journeyed to the western, northern, and southeastern coasts of South America.

Cortés's increasing wealth and power eventually aroused the deep suspicion and fear of Velásquez. It was inevitable that the governor and his erstwhile protégé would have a falling out. Velásquez was gradually cutting his ties with Hispaniola and trying to set himself up as an independent agent of the king, to whom he now quite often reported directly, bypassing his immediate superior, the viceroy of the Indies, Colón. As long as the people around Velásquez were dependent on his favor, he felt safe enough. Now, however, Velásquez began to consider Cortés's growing influence and popularity a serious threat to his supremacy.

The dispute between the two men was complicated. Officially, it centered on a woman. Catalina Juárez, a pretty Spanish girl looking for a rich husband in the Indies, was one of Cortés's many conquests, but she was different from his previous girlfriends in that she demanded his submission instead of merely giving him hers. Cortés enjoyed the affair, but marriage was not part of his plans just then.

Ordinarily this would have been a minor matter. However, it happened that Velásquez was married

An illustration from a codex, a loose-leaf book, depicting Spanish explorers with their Indian slaves. Natives enslaved by the Spanish colonialists were often treated brutally, their traditional way of life being replaced by a daily routine of hard labor on large plantations.

to one of Catalina's two sisters, and after her death became the lover of the other. Family honor was at stake here.

That was the official, public reason for the conflict. Actually, the differences between Cortés and Velásquez went deeper. Some settlers, dissatisfied with the way Velásquez distributed land, had petitioned Spain to investigate the matter. Cortés was the closest thing to a lawyer in the area, and they

Ruins of the Temple of the Warriors at Chichén-Itzá in Mexico's Yucatán Peninsula. Though the Mayans lacked iron tools, they erected many elaborately carved stone buildings.

asked him to present their case in Hispaniola. Cortés had no complaint of his own; he was doing very well. But he recognized that the dispute would give him a chance to drive a wedge between Velásquez and his people. Velásquez may have been right in fearing that the popular younger man wanted to take over his job. In any event, Cortés put the petition in good legal form and took up the case against his patron.

Velásquez, who had informers everywhere, heard about it at once. Using the affair of Catalina Juárez's honor as an excuse, he had Cortés thrown in jail. Cortés, who knew that the governor could ruin him over this charge, realized that he might be kept in chains for years, or deported back to Spain. His life as a prosperous plantation owner seemed to be in jeopardy.

Probably with the help of the jailer, Cortés managed to escape, taking refuge in a church. He knew religious law protected him from being arrested inside a church. A few days later, he made the mistake of stepping out to talk to a woman, and was arrested by a band of waiting soldiers, who clapped him in double chains and put him on a boat for Hispaniola.

A Mayan temple mural dating from a period between 1200 and 1540 shows the lifestyle of a typical Mayan village. When news reached Cuba that the nearby Yucatán Peninsula was home to an advanced and wealthy civilization—that of the Mayas— several Spanish conquistadors raced to be the first to claim the land and its riches.

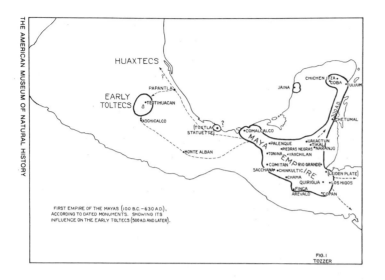

Map of the Mayan empire on the Yucatán at its height, around 600–900 A.D. By the time the Spanish began their forays on the peninsula, Mayan influence had lessened, while that of the Aztecs of central Mexico had expanded.

Once more, however, he escaped and swam to shore. Then, instead of going into hiding, Cortés went straight to Velásquez's office and asked for a pardon. Velásquez, who was facing a minor Indian uprising, needed all the friends he could get. He granted Cortés his pardon, and Cortés agreed to marry Catalina. The amicable relationship between the two rivals appeared to have been restored.

Cortés was by now one of the richest men in Cuba, and he lived like a lord. He gave grand parties, gambled freely, and generally seemed, at age 30, to have realized all his dreams. If he was restless and dissatisfied, nothing in his behavior in those days shows it.

Ships were sailing out of Cuba every day in quest of gold or slaves, but few returned much richer. Some disappeared at sea, some sailed back disappointed, a few brought back enough slaves to pay their costs. Disease and mistreatment had reduced the labor force so severely that the slave trade was a major industry in Cuba, but that sort of business did not appeal much to the prosperous Cortés.

In 1517 a report of a new discovery hit Cuba like a tropical hurricane. Explorers had found a new land, different from all the rest, and had seen sights to make even the richest Spaniard's mouth water. They had seen an advanced civilization with great temples and palaces, paved streets and bridges, and—most exciting of all—gold and silver, pearls and precious stones. That was what the Spanish had come to the New World for. Explorers had combed the area for almost three decades now, looking for quick riches. They had found lush lands and thousands of slaves, but there had been little in the way of gold or jewels to repay their efforts. Now it seemed that someone had found the land of gold at last.

Francisco Fernández de Córdoba, a rich land-owner like Cortés, had set out for the Bahamas for slaves and been blown ashore on the Yucatán peninsula of Mexico. Just as Columbus had been sure that Cuba was part of the mainland—and the wrong mainland at that—this expedition concluded that

Spanish soldiers attempt to defend themselves from stones hurled at them by Indians. Francisco Fernández de Córdoba (1475–1525), the first of the Spanish explorers who tried to establish a presence on the Yucatán, met stiff resistance from the natives.

Yucatán was an island. The story goes that when they asked the name of the place, a native answered "Tectetán," meaning "I do not understand," and the Spanish wrote it down as "Yucatán." (Another version is that the answer meant "This is a hill of yuca," the main vegetable of those parts. Whatever the Indian said, and whatever he meant by it, the answer got into the report as Yucatán and the name stuck.)

The Indians that Fernández de Córdoba had come upon were the Maya, perhaps the most highly developed of the Mexican tribes. By then the Maya had been almost completely destroyed by other, stronger tribes, but enough remained of their art and science to convince the Spanish that they had found what they had come for.

Unfortunately for the Spanish, the natives had heard about them and resisted fiercely. The expedition barely escaped back to Cuba with half its men. Fernández de Córdoba himself was wounded by a poisoned arrow and died soon after reaching home.

Despite these calamities, the stories the ill-fated expedition brought back to Cuba whetted the Spanish appetite for gold more than anything since Columbus had first told of his discovery. Velásquez began outfitting an expedition at once. He appointed his nephew Juan de Grijalva to lead it, and gave him instructions to stake a claim and return at once. Early in 1518, Grijalva set out for Mexico with four ships.

Grijalva met with the same hostility as his hapless predecessor, but he was prepared for it and handled the situation a little better. He made a few friendly contacts. He traded some glass beads, scissors, and pins for about 20,000 pesos worth of gold and jewels, officially claimed the "island" for Spain, and headed home.

The journey took longer than expected. Strong winds kept Grijalva from reaching Cuba for six months, though one of his ships got back sooner with most of the gold and some even better stories than Fernández de Córdoba's. Suspicious that his nephew might be striking out on his own as Velásquez himself had done under Colón, Velásquez sent

He was affable in his manner and a good talker, and he had twice been chosen Alcalde [mayor] of the town of Santiago Baracoa where he had settled, and in that country it is esteemed a great honor to be chosen as Alcalde.
—BERNAL DÍAZ DEL CASTILLO
Spanish soldier, historian, and participant in the Spanish conquest of Mexico, on Cortés

another expedition to bring Grijalva back.

Cristóbal de Olid, the commander of the second expedition, also took longer to return than expected, and Velásquez, now mad with impatience, began to outfit a third expedition. Yucatán was the biggest prize yet, and he was determined not to let it slip through his fingers.

The situation was complicated by the fact that several others were already claiming Yucatán. The governor of Jamaica said he had sent ships there first, and Colón, in Hispaniola, insisted that, as his father had discovered the New World, everything in it was his by royal decree. To make matters even more confusing, King Charles I of Spain (who would be elected Holy Roman Emperor Charles V in 1519) traded the rights to Yucatán to the Flemish for their support of his campaigns in Europe. No one was sure who owned the "island." The only thing everyone agreed on was the right of Europeans to take it away from the natives.

Velásquez was shrewd enough to know that if he could colonize Yucatán with his own people he would be hard to evict. He decided to send a fleet so big and powerful that no one could resist it, and to get in before anyone else. Although Velásquez had originally instructed his nephew to come right home without staying to settle Yucatán, he was bitterly disappointed that Grijalva had taken him at his word. Grijalva had opened the door to Mexico and then left with a few trinkets instead of establishing a colony. Velásquez was not going to let the next expedition make the same mistake.

Velásquez knew he had no legal right to colonize Yucatán. Somehow he had to act within the limits of his official authority. Velásquez needed a man to

Pistol owned by Holy Roman Emperor Charles V (1500–58). After he was crowned Charles I of Spain in 1516, the new ruler set his sights on the throne of the Holy Roman Empire, and control over much of Europe. The rights to the Yucatán's riches were traded by Charles to gain support for his imperial ambitions.

THE METROPOLITAN MUSEUM OF ART

Lacandone Indians, descendants of the Mayas, pictured in front of Mayan frescoes amid temple ruins, 1941. Descendants of the Mayas still make up a large part of the Yucatán's population and continue to follow many of the old Mayan traditions.

lead his expedition who would effectively secure the island for him while staying within the letter of the law. And since he had already spent a fortune on these expeditions, he needed someone who would pay most of the expenses himself. He needed someone capable and daring, but not too much so—a man who would not try to take over. Velásquez trusted no one. And yet he was not up to undertaking the expedition himself.

Velásquez finally decided to take a chance on his old friend and former employee, bound to him by ties of marriage and personal gratitude, the courageous, intelligent and resourceful mayor of the Cuban capital and one of its richest residents, Hernán Cortés.

In a long, successful life of shrewd decisions and careful calculations, Diego Velásquez never made a bigger mistake.

41

4

The Captain

The aging Velásquez protected his interests as best he could. He spelled out Cortés's duties and restrictions carefully, instructing him to do no more than search for Grijalva and Olid, claim the land for Spain, and spread the Christian faith. He was not to mistreat the Indians, take their women, or steal their gold. Nothing was said about settlement because Velásquez knew he had no authority to establish a colony.

Cortés agreed to everything, but his legal training prompted him to add one little clause to the agreement. Article 27 authorized him, in the case of emergencies, to do whatever he had to "in the service of God and their Majesties." This rather vaguely worded clause could, thought Cortés, be used to circumvent many of the restrictions in Velásquez's orders. It could be used to allow him to kill natives, set up colonies, and plunder—when necessary for God and the king. On October 23, 1518, the two men cautiously signed the agreement.

Cortés knew he had to hurry. Everyone had his eyes on Yucatán, and the voyage could be stopped at any time by the governor of Jamaica, Colón in Hispaniola, the Flemish, or the king of Spain. He

THE BETTMANN ARCHIVE

An Aztec Indian. The Aztecs, led by the mighty Montezuma II (ca. 1480–1520), were Mexico's dominant Indian power. To claim Mexico for their king, the Spanish ultimately would have to defeat the huge armies of the Aztecs.

These Italian-made steel poniards, or daggers, were the sort used by the conquistadors. The possession of such weapons gave the Europeans an enormous advantage over the natives of the New World, where the metal was yet unknown.

knew Velásquez was nervous and suspicious and might change his mind.

Everything Cortés had accumulated in the Indies went for the expedition. He obtained six ships and began collecting men and supplies as fast as he could. In four weeks, he acquired all the arms and food and barter goods he thought he would need and recruited some 300 seasoned veterans for the voyage. He mortgaged his farm and went heavily into debt. It was an all-or-nothing venture for Cortés.

This was officially to be an expedition to find their countrymen, bring word of God and the king to the heathen, and claim land, but no one was in any real doubt about what Cortés had in mind. All his men were to share in the treasures they would find, he promised. His gold-embroidered banners proclaimed, "Comrades, with true faith follow the Holy Cross and through it we shall conquer." Whatever the paper he had signed said, it was clear to his men that this was to be an expedition of conquest.

It was becoming clear to Velásquez too, and he began to waver. The pigs and chickens and beans Cortés was buying did not worry him, and he could understand the scissors, mirrors, and glass beads. But what of the cannon, crossbows, and muskets? "I don't know what Cortés's intentions are toward me," Velásquez told a friend, "but I think evil." Cortés knew he did not have much time before the governor found another captain for the expedition, and he stepped up his preparations. He inspected the food, saw that the water-casks were filled, and checked the weapons. Finally he selected 16 horses, for which he paid the enormous price of 500 pesos each. (A peso at this time was officially worth a hundredth of a pound of gold. The horses cost the equivalent of 80 pounds of gold.) These animals, first brought to the Indies on Columbus's third voyage in 1502, were to save the expedition again and again.

By the end of 1518, it was apparent to Cortés that Velásquez was thinking about finding another captain to lead the expedition. Cortés now had no choice but to proceed. On November 7, he made one

It seems most credible that our Lord God has purposefully allowed these lands [Mexico] to be discovered so that Your Majesties may be fruitful and deserving in His sight by causing these barbaric tribes to be enlightened and brought to the faith by Your hand.

—July 1519 dispatch from the Veracruz town council to Queen Juana of Spain and her son, Charles I; probably dictated by Cortés

Isla de Cuba Puerto de Santiago

In hoc signo Vinces

THE BETTMANN ARCHIVE

final purchase, spending his last peso on fresh meat, and set sail.

No sooner had Cortés departed than Velásquez sent orders for his arrest to each of the Cuban ports where he was to stop on the way to Yucatán. In each one, Cortés bribed or argued his way out. The little fleet wintered in Trinidad, picking up another 200 or so soldiers, and in February it was ready to set sail for Yucatán.

On February 9, 1519, Cortés delivered an eloquent speech to his men. They would profit by the mistakes of Córdoba and Grijalva, he assured them, using "a different way, a different reasoning, a dif-

The fleet of Cortés, bound for Mexico, sails out of the harbor of Santiago de Cuba in late 1518. Though his supposed mission—as outlined by Velásquez—was to search for the leaders of two previous expeditions, Cortés made no secret of his plans to make it a journey of conquest.

45

Italian pole arm of the type used by the conquistadors. A line of soldiers holding these long weapons was effective at protecting musketeers as they reloaded their guns.

ferent skill." And he promised them, "If you do not abandon me, as I shall not abandon you, I shall make you in a very short time the richest of all men who have crossed the seas, and of all the armies that have here made war." He justified the mission as undertaken for God and "our King and our nation." He made the expedition sound like a crusade: ". . . doubt not but that the Almighty, who has never deserted the Spaniard in his contest with the infidel, will shield you . . . for your cause is a *just cause* and you are to fight under the banner of the Cross. . . ."

The next day, February 10, Cortés and 508 soldiers set off on 11 ships to make their names and their fortunes.

They planned "a different way" from their predecessors, but not a different route. Knowing nothing of the new land they were approaching, they decided to put in first at Cozumel, an island which had been Grijalva's first stop.

One of Cortés's captains, Pedro de Alvarado, was too impatient to wait, and, sailing ahead, reached Cozumel two days before the rest of the fleet. Although the crew only stole some chickens and a few small temple ornaments from a village, their leader was furious when he arrived with the other 10 ships. He showed the "different reasoning" he planned for the expedition by throwing Alvarado's pilot, Camacho, in the brig for disobeying orders and publicly reprimanding the big red-headed captain. Then he returned all the trinkets the men had taken and, with profound apologies, paid for the chickens with barter goods. The shy natives, once they were made to understand, thought themselves lucky to get such treasures as bells, steel knives (steel was unknown in the New World), and green glass beads in return for a few chickens.

Cortés soon won the Indians' trust, and it was not hard to persuade them to give up their idols and accept Christianity—or the simplified version of Christianity that he was able to convey to them.

The Spanish learned from the Indians that other men with beards and strange clothes were being held by the Indians on the mainland. Cortés sent

Cortés addressing his men in February 1519, just before reaching the Yucatán. The speech included this promise: "I shall make you in a very short time the richest of all men who have crossed the seas. . . ."

someone to find them, and discovered two Spaniards who had been shipwrecked on a trip to Panama in 1511. Nineteen survivors of that shipwreck had drifted ashore there and been captured by the natives. The captain, Juan de Valdivia, had been sacrificed and eaten. Others had died or disappeared. Of the two remaining survivors, one had gone completely native. He now wore ear pendants, a stone plug in his lower lip, and a full ceremonial tattoo. He did not want to leave his native wife and three children, and refused to join the Spanish. The other, Jerónimo de Aguilar, a Spanish priest, had not been so willing to assimilate and had been made a slave by the Indians. He was grateful to be rescued by his own people, and, after eight years with the Maya, was able to interpret for the Spanish. As "the tongue of Cortés," he became one of the expedition's

Codex illustration depicting natives engaged in cannibalism. The captain of one Spanish expedition prior to Cortés's, after being shipwrecked and captured, had been ceremoniously sacrificed and then eaten.

Another type of Italian pole arm used by the Spanish. The weapon's long reach gave the Spanish a large advantage over the smaller clubs and spears of Indian warriors.

most valuable members.

Now that they could communicate with the natives, the adventurers crossed over to the peninsula. Aguilar went on ahead to try to persuade the natives that the Spanish wanted only to trade for food. The Mayas of the town of Tabasco had been friendly to Grijalva initially, but they were by now suspicious and refused to deal with the Spaniards. When Cortés insisted, the Tabascans warned him that if the Spanish approached, they would attack.

For Cortés, that was enough to justify an invasion. Always careful to do everything by the book, he read the articles of war to the uncomprehending tribe before he made a move. Then, with muskets and cannon, his soldiers mowed down the native troops until the corpses of Indians covered the ground. Although the Tabascans, who vastly outnumbered the Spanish, fought with great bravery, they were helpless before the onslaught. At last, Cortés played his strongest card. He led his final assault on horseback.

The Indians, who had never seen horses before, panicked at the sight. Thinking man and animal a single, supernatural monster, they threw down their slings, stones, and spears and ran screaming into the woods.

The victory brought the Spanish several rewards.

It showed them how the Indians waged war, and it earned the Spanish a reputation for invincibility that made the natives' courage seem fruitless. The shrewd Cortés capitalized on this, putting on a spectacular show of power for the vanquished Indians. With rearing horses and thundering cannon he struck such terror into the hearts of his Indian audience that he could be sure a report would reach the ears of any who might think to oppose his march.

The Tabascans embraced the Christian God with a devotion based on terror, and they showered the Spanish troops with whatever they had to offer. They gave Cortés and his men food, drink, gold, and women.

The Spanish were disappointed with the gold. They were able to collect only a few handfuls of trinkets. When they asked for more, the Indians just gestured vaguely toward the west and said "Culhúa" or "México." These were unfathomable responses, but they were all the Spanish could get out of the natives.

Because the law said that the soldiers could have no sexual relations with non-Christian women, Cortés simply had all the native women baptized, and distributed them, like the golden trinkets and the food, as spoils of war. One of these agreeable

Indians and Spanish explorers sight each other. Though the Spanish galleons and weapons were enough to subdue any Indian attack, it was their horses—creatures never before seen by Indians and perceived by them as supernatural—that gave the conquistadors an aura of invincibility.

GIRAUDON/ART RESOURCE

acquisitions was a particularly valuable addition to their number. The beautiful and regal daughter of a chief, she stood out from the others as commanding special respect. Cortés discovered that in addition to Mayan, she spoke Náhuatl, the language of the ruling tribe of the area, the Aztecs. She could interpret to Aguilar, who could put her words into Spanish for Cortés. In a short time, she learned enough Spanish herself to take Aguilar's place as the expedition's interpreter. She was baptized Marina, and her naturally aristocratic bearing earned her the title Doña among the Spanish. Since the natives could not pronounce "r," Doña Marina became Doña Malina, and the native suffix "-che" (which signified respect) was added. As "Malinche," the chieftain's daughter became so completely identified with Cortés that the natives used the name for both of them.

Malinche interpreted other things besides language for the Spanish. Her experience with various tribes of the area enabled her to explain the customs and ideas of the Indians to her captors, and she quickly became the most valuable member of the expedition. Cortés took her into his confidence completely, and eventually into his tent as well. In time, Malinche bore him a son.

When Cortés defeated the Tabascans, he cut three slashes in a tree and claimed the territory for Spain. Significantly, he said nothing in his declaration about Velásquez. Cortés considered himself accountable only to the king. Thus, Cortés did to the governor, Velásquez, just what Velásquez had done to the viceroy, Colón. He declared himself an independent agent.

Cortés knew that a declaration and a few sword slashes—however carefully recorded by the official clerk—would never really establish his claim to the new land. And he had not invested so much and come so far for a handful of gold ornaments.

So the little fleet sailed west, toward where the Tabascans had pointed when asked for more gold. On April 21, 1519, the adventurers landed at a harbor that seemed perfect for settlement, and Cortés optimistically named it Villa Rica de la Vera Cruz

("Rich Village of the True Cross"). The official founding of Veracruz, as it is now called, took place the next month with all proper ceremony. Cortés himself laid the first stone. This formal act of defiance was a turning point for Cortés. He had himself elected governor of the new territory and he appointed his friends to the city council. There was no longer even a pretense that he was an agent of Diego Velásquez. But Cortés was careful to protect himself against the long arm of the influential governor of Cuba. He sent a letter to the king of Spain, duly signed by the city council of Villa Rica de la Vera Cruz, explaining and justifying his action. With it, he sent all the gold they had accumulated—not just the "king's fifth" usually rendered to the crown—to strengthen his argument. He knew about King Charles's greed, and felt sure that this taste of gold would make him hungry for more.

Cortés was also concerned about the possibility of disloyalty among his men. Some remained faithful to Velásquez, and some thought the whole expedition was too risky. There was talk of mutiny

Map of Cortés's voyage to Mexico. After sailing from the Cuban port of Santiago and wintering in the port of Trinidad, Cortés stopped for food at the island of Cozumel. The expedition then landed on the Yucatán Peninsula, sailed to Villa Rica de la Vera Cruz, and finally pushed onward to the Aztec capital, Tenochtitlán (here shown as Mexico).

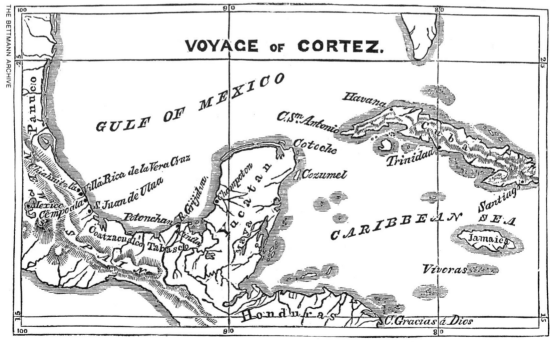

A wooden statue of a priest carved by the Tabascan Indians. The Tabascans were the first natives to face the imposing Spanish war machine. Terrified by Cortés and his army, they quickly converted to Christianity.

and returning to Cuba. Cortés had to win them over, to commit them to his own dream of conquest. He gave secret orders to bore holes in the 10 remaining ships, and spread the story that sea worms had weakened their timbers. Then he left it up to his men whether to risk a trip back or not. Cortés thus demonstrated an important aspect of his genius as a leader—an ability to make his men feel that they had made the most important decisions themselves. On this occasion, his men voted to keep going forward. There was nowhere to head but inland now, to whatever fate the silent jungle held for them.

Cortés had already seen the Aztecs, the ruling tribe of Mexico, at Veracruz. He had seen their richly decorated robes and their golden ornaments, and he knew from Malinche something of their wealth and their power. It was in their capital, if anywhere, that what the Spanish had come so far and risked so much for was to be found. So it was to that city, 200 miles inland, that Cortés now turned his attention.

We could look for no help or assistance, but that which came from God, for we no longer possessed ships in which to return to Cuba, but must rely on our own good swords and stout hearts.
—BERNAL DÍAZ DEL CASTILLO
describing the men's plight after Cortés destroyed their boats

Cortés scuttling his ships at Veracruz, 1519. When some of his men objected that the expedition was too dangerous and said they wanted to turn back, Cortés began to fear a possible mutiny. By sinking his fleet, he left them no choice but to proceed inland to face the Aztecs.

FERDINANDO CORTES
CAVATO DA VN ORIGENALE FATTO INAZI
CH'EI SI PORTASSI ALLA CONQVISTA DEL MESSICO

5

The Invader

Cortés was beginning to learn something of the people of Mexico and they were beginning to learn something of him. News of his arrival soon reached the ears of the ruler of all Mexico, Montezuma II. This mighty chieftain had been a great war leader before he became emperor of the Aztecs in 1502. His tribe had been a wandering people, poorer than most, a few centuries before, and had hired themselves out as mercenary soldiers to stronger tribes in Middle America in the 14th century. During the next 200 years they had gained control of the entire country. When Montezuma, whose full original name, Motecuzoma Xocoyotzín, meant "Courageous Young Lord," was made emperor, he commanded the greatest army ever assembled in the region.

Montezuma was the high priest of his people as well as their emperor. The Aztecs' chief deity was Huitzilopochtli, a war god who fed on fresh human hearts, and the Aztecs were tirelessly devoted to satisfying his hunger for them. Human sacrifice had become their principal goal.

The Aztec leader held his rich and powerful empire together by the force of his personality and the

Engraved portrait of Cortés. By the time of his march on Tenochtitlán, Cortés had asserted his independence from Governor Velásquez and gave his allegiance directly to the king of Spain.

THE AMERICAN MUSEUM OF NATURAL HISTORY

An Aztec leader being offered tributes by his people. The Aztecs, once a poor, nomadic tribe, established an empire that eventually spanned much of central and southern Mexico.

terror his army inspired. All the other peoples of Middle America accepted his rule and paid tributes to maintain his grand and luxurious capital, Tenochtitlán (modern-day Mexico City).

In some ways, Montezuma was as much the victim of his dreadful religion as his subjects were. When word of the strange, fair visitors with their monstrous animals and thundering cannon came to him, he was as frightened as the Tabascans had been. An Aztec legend held that another god, Quetzalcóatl ("feathered snake"), had introduced agriculture and writing to the Indians, but he had been

Montezuma II, emperor and high priest of the Aztecs. Unlike most of the rulers who preceded him, Montezuma was a poor military leader. Philosophical and superstitious, he was ill-equipped to deal with the ruthless Cortés.

Illustration depicting an Aztec feather-working technique. The Aztecs, who were great craftspeople, used feathers to decorate capes, headdresses, and shield covers.

driven away. Sailing to the east on a raft of snakes, he had promised to return and destroy the fierce death-god Huitzilopochtli.

When Montezuma learned that Cortés and his men had come from the east, he had little doubt that they were representatives of the returning Quetzalcóatl, if not the god himself with his court. Montezuma's training as a warrior-king had not prepared him to face "the fair god," much less fight him, and for the first time in his 17 years of absolute power he felt panic. Years later a native observer described the emperor as "unable to rest, to sleep, to eat." Montezuma, he reported, "would speak to no one. He seemed in great torment. He sighed. He felt weak. He could enjoy nothing. 'What will happen now?' he kept asking. 'Who will be lord as I have been now? My heart is burning. . . .' " Montezuma asked his priests what to do, but they could give him no clear answers. He wavered between submission and defiance, and tried to buy time with gifts, sending Cortés some gold and fine cotton fabric decorated with feathers, along with a message that the Spanish were to turn back from the capital.

An Aztec standard bearer, made of sandstone, dating from the late 15th century. The Aztecs worshipped many gods and decorated their temples with stone figures such as this.

Montezuma's decision was the worst he could have made, because it revealed to Cortés that the Aztecs were afraid of him, and that they had gold. Cortés sent his thanks and said that he would not be dissuaded from visiting Tenochtitlán. Montezuma then sent word that the roads were bad, there was no food for the Spanish, the emperor was sick. But every ounce of gold and every desperate excuse he sent only spurred the Spanish on.

Without the glittering prize of a city of gold dangling before them, the Spanish might well have been tempted to turn back. They were marching through dangerous and inhospitable terrain. Burning plains gave way to dense jungle. On the fourth day of the march, they reached the Sierra Madre mountains— "such an altitude there is not one in Spain more difficult to pass," according to Cortés's second report to the Spanish king. For the next three days they crossed a desert of caked mud, swept with violent sandstorms and watered only by salt lakes.

Rattlesnakes, scorpions, poisonous spiders, and mosquitoes almost accomplished what Montezuma's messages failed to do, and the Spaniards were becoming discouraged. There was even talk of turning back. The Spaniards' spirits revived, however, when they came at last to the city of Cempoala. There they found the largest community they had yet seen—a place of "gardens and greenery and well-watered orchards" with stucco houses so brilliantly whitewashed that the first soldiers who saw the buildings thought they were made of silver.

Cempoala was the capital of the province of Totonacán, once a rich, independent kingdom which the Aztecs had conquered. Its chief, Chicomacatl, a man so fat he could barely walk, greeted Cortés and his men warmly with flowers and incense, and revealed that his people were bitterly unhappy under Aztec rule. This was the opening Cortés had been hoping for, the first real evidence of Aztec disunity. He lost no time in urging Chicomacatl, who was known as the Fat Chief, to rebel. The Spanish had come, Cortés assured him, to bring peace and prosperity to his people, the Totonacs, and to bring an end to the tyranny of the Aztecs.

[The Aztecs] said that by no means would they give themselves up, for as long as one of them was left he would die fighting, and that we would get nothing of theirs because they would burn everything or throw it into the water.
—HERNÁN CORTÉS
letter to King Charles

The Fat Chief was uncertain about so daring a move. He became even more unwilling to join the Spanish when Cortés's priest demanded that the Totonacs give up their religious practice of human sacrifice. "At that time," according to historian Hammond Innes, the Cempoalans "were regularly sacrificing . . . up to five humans a day, offering up their hearts to the idols and eating the arms and legs."

While the amiable Fat Chief procrastinated, Cortés saw a chance to force his hand. Five Aztec tax collectors arrived in Cempoala to exact their usual tribute of gold, women, and sacrificial victims, and Cortés took the great risk of having them arrested. The Totonacs, realizing that Montezuma's punishment for such audacity would be dreadful, were terrified, and finally concluded that they had no choice but to throw in their lot with these god-like Spaniards. Then the Fat Chief submitted, accepted the sovereignty of the king of Spain, and gave Cortés 1,000 men to continue his march.

Cortés knew that all these events were being closely observed by Montezuma's spies, and he continued his double game. He sent the tax collectors back to the Aztecs with the message that he had rescued them from the rebellious Cempoalans. He wanted nothing but to make peace in the region, Cortés said, and to do so he and his men would have to come to Tenochtitlán.

Montezuma sent gifts of gold and cloth, as usual, but he no longer really believed that the Spanish could be bribed to leave. However, he knew that they were human now, and hoped that they might yet be defeated. If they could not be ambushed on the way, they could be trapped in Tenochtitlán.

Cortés now rode at the head of a large native army, supported by 50 Totonac villages. When he reached the city of Xocotlán—which was ruled by a chief even fatter than the Fat Chief—he came as a conqueror. But the Shaker, as the Spanish called the chief of Xocotlán, was unimpressed. He refused cooperation unless ordered by his emperor, Montezuma, who, he said, commanded 30 great lords who among them commanded 3 million men. The Shaker gave

It seems to me that we have already gained a great reputation for valour throughout this country, and that from what they saw us do in the matter of Montezuma's tax-gatherers, the people here take us for gods or beings like their idols.

—HERNÁN CORTÉS

them food—"very little of it, and . . . given with ill will" according to Cortés's chronicler, Bernal Díaz—and advised them to make their way to Tenochtitlán through the friendly religious center of Cholula.

The Spanish were undaunted by the prospect of attacking an empire that possessed such vast armies. God, in whose name they never ceased to insist their expedition was being conducted, had been with them so far, and would not fail them now. The sight of 13 temples decorated with a total of 100,000 skulls only steeled them to their task of overturning this savage religion and firmly planting the cross and the banner of their king on Mexican soil.

The Totonacs were their loyal friends now, and

The Aztecs made human sacrifice an important part of their religious rituals, and skulls were often used to decorate their shrines. Such practices revolted the Spanish, who viewed them as further evidence of the Aztecs' "need" for Christianity.

UPI/BETTMANN NEWSPHOTOS

advised them against heading for Cholula. The Cholulans, they said, were treacherous, and the Spanish would surely be slaughtered and eaten if they set foot in it. And Cholula was in the center of Culhúa, the fiercest and most loyal province of the Aztec empire. The Spanish should keep to their original route, their new friends urged, and go by way of Tlascala, whose people were old allies of the Totonacs and enemies of Montezuma.

Since it seemed that none of the Indians of Mexico could be trusted to tell the truth, Cortés was not sure which tribe was trying to trick him. The Shaker was certainly no friend, but Montezuma sent repeated messages to Cortés, warning him not to trust the Totonacs either. At last the Spanish chose the harder path through Tlascala as the safer way.

Tlascala was a well-defended federation of Indian villages which had long resisted Montezuma and might be looked to for support in Cortés's venture. But they had heard of the Spaniard's cordial communications with the emperor and were, as Montezuma hoped, suspicious of them.

Cortés repeatedly sent messages of peace, but the Tlascalans massed an army of 50,000 men to oppose the Spanish. Horses were useless against the Tlascalans' most fearsome weapon—the *macatl*, a powerful sword wider at the tip than at the base and edged with flakes of obsidian. With this weapon the Aztecs could sever an unarmored limb or decapitate a horse at a single blow. The Spanish took severe losses. In open country, their cannon were effective and scattered the Tlascalans, but nothing seemed to discourage the native warriors. Cortés saw that he was gradually losing ground. He himself became ill, and most of his men were also sick or wounded.

Cortés knew that unless he secured Tlascala he could never get through to Tenochtitlán, and he tried every means to bring the campaign to an end. He released all prisoners with kind words, gifts, and assurances that all he wanted was free passage through Tlascala, but the enemy was implacable. Díaz reports one Tlascalan captain's response to a bid for peace: "The reply was . . . that we might go to his town where his father was living; that there

> *He told them [the Mexican Indians] many things about our holy religion as well stated as only a priest could do it nowadays, so that it was listened to with good will.*
> —BERNAL DÍAZ DEL CASTILLO

peace would be made by satiating themselves on our flesh, and honor paid to their gods with our hearts and blood, and that we should see his answer the very next day."

The Spanish were running out of food, too, and were living on game and the small dogs the Indians raised for meat. They buried their dead secretly at night, so the enemy would not see that they were mortals, and doctored the wounded with oil rendered from the fat of a fallen Tlascalan's body.

For three weeks the battle raged, and the Spanish began to lose heart. They were badly outnumbered, and the enemy knew they were mortal. But just as things were beginning to look their worst, a ray of hope appeared. Dissension seemed to be developing in the Tlascalan ranks, and some of the chiefs approached the Spanish camp seeking to make peace on their own.

Tlascalan women appeared in camp with gifts and a message from the leader of the Indians. "If you are savage gods," the message said, "take these four women and sacrifice them, and you can eat their flesh and hearts. . . . But if you are men, eat the poultry and the bread and the fruit. And if you are gentle gods, here are feathers and incense; make your sacrifice with that." The next day, 50 more Tlascalans came to the camp with food.

Glad as they were for the turkeys and cherries and tortillas, the Spanish were suspicious of the messengers. Malinche, always a great help in such situations, listened to the messengers' conversations among themselves and quickly discovered that they were spies gathering information for a Tlascalan night attack. She went to Cortés with the news.

Cortés questioned the natives and learned that the information was correct. Then he rounded up 17 of the spies, cut off the hands of some and the thumbs of others, and sent the men back with a stern message for their leaders. The Tlascalans, he said, were to "quit their foolishness and make peace." As Prescott recounts, Cortés warned the Indians that no matter whether they came "by day or night; they would find the Spaniards ready for them." When the attack came, the Tlascalan war-

We fought so hard that in two hours more than 3,000 men were killed.
—HERNÁN CORTÉS
from a 1519 letter to King Charles of Spain describing the Cholula massacre

riors were easily routed. After three more days of dispirited fighting, the Tlascalan chief and 50 of his captains came to beg for peace. They pledged their undying support to Cortés and became his staunchest allies.

Like the Cempoalans and Tabascans, the Tlascalans were almost slavish in their newfound devotion to the Spanish. They were even more bitter about Aztec domination than the other tribes the Spanish had met, and saw Cortés as the long-awaited leader who could free them. Cortés did nothing to discourage this view. Tlascala was a city of some 30,000 people—bigger than Granada, in Spain—and controlled a much larger area yet. The Tlascalans offered 10,000 soldiers to Cortés's growing army.

The success of Cortés's Tlascalan campaign completely demoralized Montezuma. Once again, he sent ambassadors with gifts to Cortés, and congratulated him on his victory, warning him not to trust the treacherous Tlascalans. He would accept the authority of the Spanish crown, he said, and send whatever tribute was required in gold, jewels, fabric, feathers, or sacrificial victims, if the Spanish would only leave.

Before Cortés could reply to this latest entreaty, Montezuma inexplicably reversed his policy and invited the Spanish to visit him. The best route, he suggested, would be through the holy city of Cholula, where a welcome was being prepared for the Spanish. There, he said, they could rest and prepare for the trip to Tenochtitlán. The Tlascalans in turn warned Cortés against the treachery of the Aztecs and told him, as the Cempoalans had done, that Cholula would be a trap.

The wily Cortés thanked Montezuma's ambassadors warmly and sent back gifts and compliments. He also listened carefully to the counsel of his Tlascalan and Cempoalan advisers. The name Cortés means "courteous" in Spanish, and the commander never ceased to live up to it. He was becoming as skillful a diplomat as he was a soldier, and learning how to play the Indians' game as well as they.

After some parleying with the Cholulan leaders,

In the illustration:
ycmoquayateq que tlatoque

A codex illustration depicting the baptism of four Tlascalan chiefs. Looking on are Cortés (seated right of center, holding crucifix) and, at his side, Malinche, his mistress-interpreter. The legend reads "thus the chiefs were baptized."

Cortés accepted their gracious invitation and marched to the city—a great metropolis of over 100,000 people with nearly 400 temples. The Spanish were treated well when they arrived, as Montezuma had promised, and enjoyed the luxury of good food and spacious, comfortable accommodation for a few days. But they soon became alarmed as the women and children moved quietly out to the mountains, and the amiable Cholulans began to talk secretly among themselves.

Malinche was busy making friends among the women, and one chief's wife wanted her to stay and marry one of her sons. It was the only way she could save herself, the matron told her, because an ambush was planned, on the emperor's orders, for the next day.

65

The quick-witted girl agreed to the marriage, but went straight to Cortés with the story. The Spanish commander had left his men—Spanish, Cempoalan, and Tlascalan—strategically placed inside the city and around it. He gave orders to lock up the Cholulan leaders, called the surprised warriors into the main square, and gave a signal. As the shot rang out, Spanish guns and crossbows were turned on Cholulans. The chief warriors were slain at once, and without leaders the Cholulans were helpless.

The holy city of Cholula was ravaged. Cempoalan spear and Tlascalan *macatl* finished what Spanish cannon and sword had begun, and in hours more than 6,000 Cholulans lay dead in the streets. For two days the Spaniards and their allies continued their bloody work, hacking the stunned survivors to pieces, burning the priests in their temples, and pulling down the fine homes of the nobles.

Señor Malinche, I understand what you have said about three gods and the cross, but here we have always worshipped our own gods and thought they were good, as no doubt yours are.

—MONTEZUMA
speech to Cortés, as quoted
by Bernal Díaz del Castillo

Once Cortés had made his point, he set about restoring order and helping the few Cholulans who had escaped to rebuild their shattered city. He made peace between them and the Tlascalans, and bound both tribes to the service of his king. Within weeks the market place was busy again and Cortés had an army so great that even the dreaded Aztec force might tremble at it.

Montezuma turned to prayer and sacrificed fresh victims to Huitzilopochtli, even though the god seemed to be failing him. Then he sent his ambassadors to Cholula with gifts for his "good friend" Cortés and protested his indignation at the "evil and lying" Cholulans. Again, he offered gold.

Cortés thanked Montezuma profusely, sent him a string of glass beads, and reassured him of his love and respect. Then he resumed his relentless march on Tenochtitlán.

The Spanish conquest of Mexico entailed one bloody slaughter after another. Those Indians who survived Cortés's massacres eagerly became his allies. In this way, Cortés eventually built an army that was strong enough to challenge that of Montezuma.

6

The Guest

With such wonderful sights to gaze on, we did not know what to say, or if what we saw before our eyes was real.
—BERNAL DÍAZ DEL CASTILLO
recording the reactions of Cortés's men to the splendor of Tenochtitlán

The Cholulans, after plotting to kill the Spanish by stealth and then suffering a bloody massacre at their hands, joined forces with Cortés's men and marched loyally at their side against the Aztecs. But now that the campaign was entering its final and most dangerous phase, the Cempoalans lost heart and asked to withdraw. Cortés, ever the diplomat, sent them home with his thanks and rich gifts.

The 400 or so remaining Spaniards were confident enough without the Cempoalans. Their victories at Tabasco, Tlascala, and Cholula had almost led them to share the natives' belief in their supernatural powers, and they now marched among thousands of Indian allies.

The confidence of the Spanish grew even greater as it became clear that Montezuma was becoming desperate. The Aztec emperor alternately invited the Spanish to visit and ordered them to leave, expressed humble reverence and threatened violent resistance, gave stern commands and pleaded for mercy.

The Spanish rested for three weeks in Cholula. Then, on November 1, 1519, they set out on their final march, passing through desert and mountain

THE AMERICAN MUSEUM OF NATURAL HISTORY

Reception of Cortés by Montezuma in Tenochtitlán in 1519. The Aztec leader believed Cortés to be Quetzalcóatl, lord of creation and the enemy of the Aztecs' war god. Montezuma repeatedly tried to thwart Cortés's approach to the city, but he treated the Spaniard with great honor when he arrived.

THE BETTMANN ARCHIVE

Aztec frog stamp found at Teotihuacán, one of the great Aztec religious centers. This ancient city dominated much of Mexico for over seven centuries.

country, rallying support at each village. Twenty miles from Cholula they passed between the twin volcanoes Ixtaccíhuatl and Popocatépetl, which stand like sentinels guarding the capital.

The closer Cortés advanced, the more piteous Montezuma's messages to him became. The priest-king probably saw the encroachers as at least agents of the old rejected god Quetzalcóatl, who had promised to return and end the cruel worship of Huitzilopochtli. Whether or not Montezuma believed that Cortés was a god, he must have seen that the cult of Huitzilopochtli—and with it the religious basis of his empire—could not stand up to the Spanish. As R. C. Padden, a historian of Aztec religion, explains in his book *The Hummingbird and the Hawk*: "Without the threat of sacrifice there would be no discipline, and the empire could not exist 24 hours without . . . terror. In the absence of fear, Huitzilopochtli could not survive."

Montezuma had done everything within his power to ward off the Spanish advance. He had tried threats and bribery, commands and pleas, lies and truth. He had offered prayers and sacrifices, sent armies to fight, and arranged an ambush. But the Spanish had prevailed. Their strange clothes and language, their beards and fair skin, their giant animals and thundering weapons which could deal unseen death at a distance—all of these things were clear evidence to the Aztecs that the Spanish were no mere men.

Gathering strength from the Indians' panic, the Spanish marched on to Tenochtitlán, the jewel in the crown of the Aztec empire.

First settled in 1325, this beautiful metropolis in the center of Mexico was equal in grandeur to anything in Europe. Cortés reported that it numbered as many as 100,000 occupied houses "as good as the best in Spain . . . in size and workmanship," and modern estimates of its population range from 90,000 to 1 million. Even allowing for the exaggerations of its conquerors, it must have been—as it is today—one of the largest cities in the world. The population of London at that time was about 40,000, and that of Paris 65,000.

Spanish map of Tenochtitlán. Tenochtitlán was considered the "jewel" in the Aztec crown, a city of towering temples and great palaces, of orchards and flower gardens; At the time of Cortés's conquest Tenochtitlán was more populous than London and Paris.

Tenochtitlán was built on an island in Lake Texcoco. The city's towering temples and great palaces of polished stone seemed to rise out of the salt water of the lake like something in a dream. A city of orchards and flower gardens, it was dotted with ponds of fresh water filled with fish and ducks. In the lake around it, flowers, fruit, and vegetables grew on *chinampas*—man-made islands which the Spanish called "floating gardens." Great double-channeled aqueducts carried fresh water across the salt lake by an intricate system of engineering seldom equalled in any civilization.

Three wide causeways, on which eight men could ride abreast, joined Tenochtitlán to the shore. Canoes passed among the *chinampas* and larger islands in the lake, and in the many interconnected smaller causeways there were wooden bridges which could be removed to protect the city from invasion. As the Spanish rode up to the gates of Tenochtitlán on November 8, 1519, their confidence may have flagged a little. They began to realize that the city would be hard to enter if the Aztecs wanted to defend it—and hard to escape from once they got in. "As for us," wrote Díaz, "we did not even number 400 soldiers! And we well remembered the warnings that we had been given that we should beware of entering the city, where they would kill us as soon as they had us inside. . . . What men in all the world have shown such daring?" For Cortés and his followers, however, it was too late for second thoughts. The little troop marched bravely up to the entrance of the city and waited to see what sort of a welcome they would receive.

The causeway was filled with awed and curious Aztecs watching silently as the Spanish arrived. Richly dressed nobles greeted the visitors solemnly, each touching the ground with his hand and then kissing it. After nearly an hour of this ceremonious welcome, the emperor arrived, borne in a golden litter encrusted with jewels. He too touched the ground and kissed his hand in formal welcome to Cortés.

The two leaders met and exchanged necklaces. Cortés assured Montezuma, through Malinche, that

> *Be assured that we shall obey you. All that we own is yours to dispose of. You are in your own country and your own house.*
> —MONTEZUMA
> Aztec emperor, to Cortés,
> Nov. 1519

he had not come as a conqueror but as a friend, one who loved and respected him and wished him well. The emperor, now resigned, told the Spaniard that he accepted the authority of the king of Spain. "In all the land that lies in my domain," he sadly said, "you may command as you will, for you shall be obeyed."

The Spaniards saw the Aztecs as godless barbarians, devilish in their religion and savage in their behavior, but they were much impressed by the emperor. Díaz wrote: "The great Montezuma was about 40 years old, of good height and well proportioned, slender and spare of flesh, not very swarthy. . . . His face was somewhat long, but cheerful, and he had good eyes and showed in his appearance and manner both tenderness and, when necessary, gravity. He was very clean and bathed once every day." More impressive yet was his generosity. The Spanish were shown to spacious quarters, served "a sumptuous dinner," and given women to wait on them. Then the emperor presented each officer with gifts of gold and three loads of cotton mantles. Each soldier was given two loads of mantles.

Montezuma and Cortés "simultaneously paid reverence to one another," Díaz reported, and the soldiers were received not only as honored guests but as the lords of the city. It appeared that the conquest had succeeded without a blow being struck.

During the next few weeks, the Spanish had the opportunity to observe their hosts closely. The Aztecs appeared to them a strange blend of high civilization and savage barbarism. They had a complex, organized government, magnificent architecture, superlative art, and a calendar more accurate than the European one. In other ways, however, they were still very primitive. They had no schools, for example, and though they could send messages by a picture system, like the North American Indians, they had no written language. They cast copper and gold with great skill—in fact, they valued gold only for ornaments—but they never discovered the use of iron. They bred dogs to eat but had domesticated no other animal, and had developed no means of transport except carrying things

That night our allies dined sumptuously, for all those they had killed were sliced up and eaten.
—HERNÁN CORTÉS
after an ambush of
over 500 Aztecs

Cortés and his retinue on one of the causeways leading into Tenochtitlán. The city was built on an island in Lake Texcoco.

on their own backs. They had discovered the wheel, but used it only for toys.

The Aztec diet was incredibly varied and refined, though much of it sounds disgusting to us today. According to Díaz, they ate "almost anything that lives": snakes and dogs were among their favorite foods, along with mice, worms, lice and other insects, dried sea scum, and lizards. An account of a typical dinner served to Montezuma occupies two full pages of Díaz's history. The meal included more than 30 main courses, served over small pottery lamps to keep them warm, with more than 300 plates for the emperor to choose from. "Fowls, turkeys, pheasants, partridges, quail, tame and wild ducks, venison, wild boar, reed birds, pigeons, hares and rabbits" were among the meats served to the emperor daily. "I have heard it said," the chronicler adds cautiously, "that they cooked for him the flesh of young children, but . . . we could not see if [that was true.]" After dinner, the emperor sipped chocolate, "all frothed up, as they make it in Mexico," and watched his clowns and dancers and jugglers perform. Then he washed his hands in water brought with much ceremony by four high-born ladies, inhaled the smoke of "certain herbs which they call *tabaco*," and fell asleep.

The Spanish admired and enjoyed the many splendors of the city—Montezuma's great aviary and zoo, built long before such things were thought of in Europe; the flower gardens and wide, white avenues; and the teeming marketplace. But the Spanish were not comfortable. It had all been too easy, and they could not be sure that they had really taken the city unless they held it by force of arms. The Aztecs were gracious and respectful to them, but who could know what these impassive natives were

Cortés and Montezuma greet each other in Tenochtitlán amid elaborate ceremony in 1519. Montezuma readily acknowledged the king of Spain's authority over Mexico, while Cortés, for his part, said he had come as a friend, not as a conqueror. The two maintained a somewhat strange, friend-yet-foe relationship.

thinking? The Spanish realized that Montezuma could have them all killed in a moment. The Tlascalans, stationed outside the city, would never be able to get to their aid in time if the bridges were drawn up. The Spanish were at the mercy of their Aztec hosts.

The one feature of Aztec civilization that most horrified the Spanish was its religion. Ritual human sacrifice and cannibalism were practiced on a larger scale in Tenochtitlán than elsewhere, and there were historical accounts of celebrations in which as many as 20,000 human hearts had been ripped out of the breasts of captives to feed the hungry war god. The first visit of the Spanish to the high temple of Huitzilopochtli almost led to violence, and put a great, and lasting, strain on their relations with the Aztecs. Díaz vividly describes his first sight of the giant idol: "He had . . . monstrous and terrible eyes, and the whole of his body was covered with precious stones, and gold and pearls, and . . . was girdled by great snakes made of gold. In one hand he held a bow and in the other some arrows. . . . [He] had around his neck some Indians' faces and . . . hearts, the former made of gold and the latter of silver. . . . There were braziers, and in them [the Aztecs] were burning the hearts of three Indians whom they had sacrificed that day. . . . All the walls were so splashed and encrusted with blood that they were black, the floor was the same, and the whole place stank vilely. The walls were so clotted with blood . . . that in the slaughter houses of Spain there is not such another stench."

When Cortés called the war gods "devils," Montezuma was offended. "Señor Malinche," he replied (Cortés was always known to the emperor by this name), "if I had known you would have said such things, I would not have shown you my gods. We consider them to be very good, for they give us health and rains and good seed times. . . . We are obliged to worship them and make sacrifices, and I pray you not to say another word to their dishonor."

Seeing that he had overstepped his bounds, Cortés apologized. But he never stopped trying to

Sometimes at meal-times there were present some very ugly humpbacks, very small of stature and their bodies almost broken in half, who are their jesters, and other Indians, who must have been buffoons, who told him witty sayings, and others who sang and danced, for Montezuma was fond of pleasure and song.
—BERNAL DÍAZ DEL CASTILLO
describing Montezuma's court

persuade the emperor to accept Christianity. Finally, Montezuma grew impatient and begged Cortés to stop talking about it. But Cortés had come to Mexico as much to convert the heathen as to win gold and glory. To win a country for his Christian king, he had to win its people and their emperor for Christianity.

One day, on a visit to the main temple, Cortés became so disgusted by the human blood in the mouths and on the bodies of the idols that, to the horror of the Aztec priests, he smashed an iron bar against the face of an idol. "We must risk something for God," he cried.

Relations between the Spanish and the Aztecs deteriorated rapidly as a result of this incident. The crisis broke when Cortés learned that Aztecs had attacked his base at Veracruz.

Cortés moved swiftly. With about 30 men and his interpreters, he marched into the emperor's private

Aztec figures made of gold. The lure of such riches—more than religious fervor or conquest itself—was what had led Cortés and his men across dangerous seas and rugged terrain to the ramparts of Tenochtitlán.

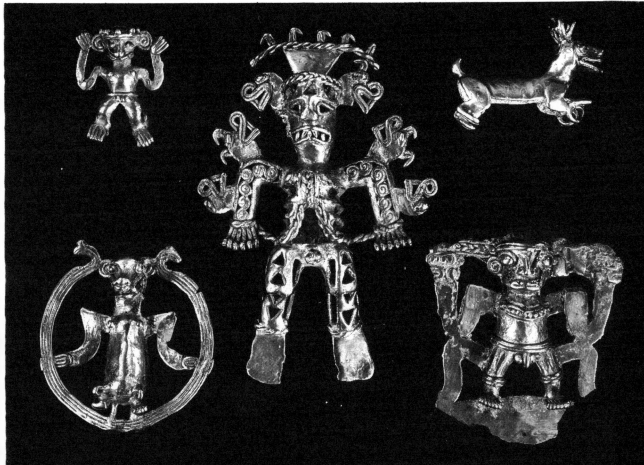

apartment and ordered Montezuma to return with them to their quarters as a guarantee of the safety of the Spanish. The emperor, furious at this threat to his royal person, refused to go.

It was a tense moment. A word from Montezuma could have brought his guards streaming down on the Spanish from every part of the palace, and the rest of his people would have turned on them in minutes. Cortés and Montezuma stood face to face for a time. The Aztec offered gold, he offered his children as hostages, but the stern-faced Spaniard would not relent. Finally, one of Cortés's officers shouted: "Let's either take him or kill him!"

The emperor surrendered. He became a prisoner in his own palace, and the power of the Aztec empire passed into the hands of Hernán Cortés.

The leaders of the Veracruz attack were swiftly brought to Tenochtitlán for trial. Montezuma, his spirit broken, turned them over to the Spanish, who quickly extracted full confessions from them all. Then, in compliance with Spanish law, the 17 nobles were burned alive, in public, under the window of the emperor's rooms. Just to make their point doubly clear to their hosts, the Spanish used the weapons the Aztecs had stored in their temples for firewood.

Cortés had all along maintained the diplomatic fiction that Montezuma was their host, and that he was staying with his guests by choice. A strange friendship had in fact grown between the two men, who played games together and often embraced. Each used terms of respect in speaking to the other, and after Cortés had taken his kingdom, the emperor was given every freedom except that of leaving the palace in which the Spanish were quartered. He had his women, his state visits with ambassadors, his luxurious diet, his daily bath, and his royal robes. He could come and go as he liked—within the confines of his prison house.

But when the time came to watch—and be seen watching—the public execution of the Veracruz rebels, Montezuma was not allowed to stand alone. With just a word to his people, who were gathered in the square below his window, Montezuma could

Montezuma sipping chocolate, one of the Aztec delicacies previously unknown to the Spanish. Montezuma's gifts to his Spanish guests of fine food, gold, and beautiful women only made the conquerors suspicious. They were uneasy about having taken Tenochtitlán without a fight.

have turned the whole city against the Spanish. Cortés decided that he would have to put his royal host in irons. With his own hand, he fixed the chains to Montezuma's arms and legs.

This was the last blow to the proud spirit of Montezuma. Cortés had discovered the one thing needed to reduce the Aztec ruler to complete subservience— the touch of iron to his wrists and ankles. When he gently removed the chains after the execution and told Montezuma that he might go back to his own palace, the Aztec humbly asked to stay with the Spanish. Indian fatalism, shame at having surrendered to the Spanish, fear of the anger of his war chiefs, a lingering belief that these visitors might be agents of the gods and could not be defied—all of these might have played a part in Montezuma's docility, but the final humiliation of his shackles finished the job.

The Spanish discovered the vast Aztec treasury in a secret room in their own quarters, and greedily melted down the gold ornaments and sacred statues into ingots. Cortés took his own share, and the king's fifth was set aside next. Then the rest was divided up among the soldiers. There was considerable dissatisfaction about the distribution. The common soldiers ended up with the equivalent of about $100 each for all their work and risk. Many of them complained of the greed of Cortés. But, as usual, the suave Spaniard smoothed everything over with a gift here, a promise there, and a rousing speech for all. It cheered everyone up for a while to be rich, but their high spirits did not last. Gold was of no use to them in Tenochtitlán, and there did not seem to be any way out of the city.

The Spanish realized that Montezuma's surrender was no guarantee of their own security. The Aztecs were angry at the desecration of their temples and no longer feared the Spanish as gods. By April 1520, it had become clear that the Indians were preparing an attack. The Spanish, recognizing that even the help of the emperor could not save them from such an onslaught, began looking for a way to slip out of the city, using Montezuma as a hostage.

Even as the Spanish prepared to depart from Te-

Codex illustration showing the Aztec religious rite in which a live human heart is ripped out of the chest and fed to the hungry war god, Huitzilopochtli. The Spanish were shocked to discover such practices.

nochtitlán, a new disaster struck. Word reached Cortés that a great fleet of Spanish ships had landed at Veracruz—not to render the aid he so desperately needed, but to arrest him and hang him as a traitor. His old friend and kinsman Velásquez had caught up with him at last.

The governor of Cuba had heard of Cortés's successes in Mexico and was furious that such a prize had eluded him. He had outfitted a fleet of 18 ships, manned them with 900 men—almost the full fighting force of Cuba—and equipped them with 12 cannon and 18 horses. He put this army under his deputy, Pánfilo de Narváez, and gave orders that Cortés was to be seized and executed. To make matters worse for Cortés, Montezuma had learned of the expedition and sent his usual gifts of gold and mantles to Narváez, inviting him to come to Tenochtitlán and carry out his assignment.

Cortés had to act fast. He knew Narváez had a rope waiting for him. As always, he tried diplomacy first. He wrote a friendly letter reminding him that they were compatriots and should stand together as a good example to the savages. When that failed, he offered to permit Narváez to share in the great riches of Mexico. But the offer was greeted with a sneer. Finally, Cortés prepared once again to fight.

Leaving Pedro de Alvarado in charge of Tenochtitlán and the emperor, Cortés set out to meet the enemy with about a third of his entire force—70 men and five horses.

Although they were underequipped and heavily outnumbered, Cortés and his men had one big advantage. They were all seasoned veterans who knew the country and how to fight in it. They made a sudden night attack on Narváez's camp near Cempoala during a tropical rainstorm and so surprised their adversaries that they panicked. The battle was brief. Narváez lost an eye to one of the long Indian lances Cortés's men had learned to use so effectively, and his troops gave up the fight. Narváez was sent back to Veracruz in chains, and most of his soldiers eagerly joined Cortés.

The army that returned to Tenochtitlán on June 24, 1520, was larger and far better supplied than

THE AMERICAN MUSEUM OF NATURAL HISTORY

Modern lacquered mask from the Tabascan Indians of Mexico. The fearsome look of Aztec crafts and religious art must have convinced Cortés that the Indians worshipped devils and should be converted to Christianity.

Cortés ministers to affairs of state as head of the Aztec empire. Cortés had usurped actual power from Montezuma by making the Aztec leader a prisoner in his own palace.

the expedition that had originally come to Yucatán 14 months before. However, the improved condition of his forces was to be of little help to Cortés. Upon arriving back in Tenochtitlán, he discovered that the city was in armed revolt against Alvarado, whose troops had slaughtered its leading citizens with swords, pikes, and muskets during a religious ceremony. The streets were deserted as Cortés entered at the head of a frightened troop of Spaniards. The Aztecs were massing for an attack.

The Spanish rode through the main square over the bodies of the 600 Aztec nobles Alvarado had massacred. Montezuma sent timid greetings, but Cortés knew about his support of Narváez and rebuffed the messenger, calling the emperor a dog. He had no time for courtesies now. Every moment had to be spent organizing a defense.

On June 25, 1520, the Aztecs swept down on the Spaniards from all sides. The Spanish artillery poured fire and death into the massed Indians. Spanish steel flashed against the padded cotton of Aztec armor, and wave after wave of native warriors fell. But still the Aztecs came on.

Stones showered from the rooftops, crippling horses and men, and the sky was black with arrows. A small Spanish force cut its way through 5,000 shouting Aztecs to the top of the great pyramid of Huitzilopochtli and set fire to the idols there, hoping to frighten the natives, but the action only enraged them all the more. The Spanish were barely able to get back to the palace that night.

A new spirit reigned among the Aztecs now. The passive, fatalistic Indians had been stirred to rebellion by a new war chief, Montezuma's brother Cuitláhuac, who had been elected emperor in Montezuma's place. The Aztecs were ready to sacrifice their lives to rid themselves of the hated Spanish. They made it clear when Cortés tried to negotiate with them that they no longer believed the Spanish were gods, and offered Cortés and his men only two choices: to die in battle or to surrender and be sacrificed to Huitzilopochtli. Neither prospect appealed much to the Spanish—especially when the Aztecs added the promise that after they had ripped the Spaniards' hearts out, they would cut off their heads to display them in the temple, chop off their arms and legs to eat, and feed their mutilated remains to the animals in the royal zoo.

The Aztecs had torn down the bridges linking their city to the mainland. There was no escape route for the Spanish. Their only chance was to try to talk their way out using the former emperor as their spokesman.

The sick and despondent Montezuma, though convinced that such a ploy would not work, agreed to negotiate on the Spaniards' behalf. "I think you will all die," he glumly predicted. He stepped out on his balcony to ask the angry Indians to let the Spanish go in peace. The natives were out for blood, however, and began pelting the balcony with stones. Three of them struck Montezuma, one on the head,

Codex illustration showing the Spanish and Indians fighting. Note the difference in weaponry: the Spanish use cannon and crossbow, while the Indians have only primitive spears.

and he fell to the floor.

The emperor's Spanish captors, who had grown genuinely fond of him, tried to bind his wounds, but he waved all help away. He had no further desire to live. Three days later, the mighty Montezuma Xocoyotzín, the Courageous Young Lord, died. For the first time since his childhood, Cortés openly shed tears. He had lost a royal hostage, a powerful foe—and a respected friend.

Cortés had also lost his last hope of a peaceful withdrawal from Tenochtitlán. He determined on a desperate scheme. He ordered his carpenters to build a portable bridge to get them across the gaps in the causeway. Then he made plans to leave the city in the middle of the night.

The Spanish attack Tenochtitlán's Great Temple, in June 1520. The Aztecs repulsed this raid, during which the Spanish set fire to the Aztec idols. Cortés eventually fled the city.

On the rainy night of June 30, 1520, the ragged remainder of the Spanish expedition began softly to steal out of Tenochtitlán. They crossed the first gap in silence, and it appeared that they might make it. Then a piercing whistle shattered the stillness, and they were surrounded by Aztec warriors who had been waiting in the dark for them.

Cortés's old veterans had had enough foresight to travel light, and most of them managed to escape the city. But Narváez's men had weighed themselves down with as much of Montezuma's gold as they could carry. Unable to run, they were helpless and nearly 100 of them were struck down or captured at once.

That night of June 30—still known as *noche triste* ("sorrowful night")—cost the Spanish over half their army and nearly all their Tlascalan friends.

The death of Montezuma at the hands of his subjects, June 1520. The Aztec leader had agreed to negotiate Cortés's safe passage out of the city but the natives, enraged at the destruction the Spanish had done, pelted Cortés's men with stones and arrows.

THE BETTMANN ARCHIVE

Several of Montezuma's children, taken on the retreat as hostages, were killed in the confusion.

The next morning found the little band of Spanish survivors physically and emotionally exhausted. Cortés rested beneath an ancient cypress, still pointed out to tourists in Mexico, and learned how many of his brave companions had fallen. Looking back at Tenochtitlán and the failure of his dream, the tough Spanish soldier wept openly for the second time that week.

The Great Temple of Tenochtitlán. This magnificent structure, which symbolized Aztec power, became the focus of Cortés's attempts to defeat the "barbarian devil-worshippers." It is said that some 20,000 humans were sacrificed at ceremonies marking the dedication of this temple.

85

7

The Conqueror

The Aztecs were determined not to let the Spanish escape, and poured out of their city after them. On the second night of the retreat, Cortés lost 150 men and 50 horses to Indian arrows and lances. The Spanish stumbled on in terror, hiding where they could, fighting when they had to, hoping to reach their camp in Tlascala. It took a week to reach the small town of Otumba, less than half of the 90-mile journey, and every day their numbers dwindled.

In the plains outside Otumba, the Spanish found themselves faced with their greatest threat yet. The field was covered on every side by fierce Aztec warriors—an army of tens of thousands stretching to the horizon, sweeping toward them with lances leveled. They were surrounded. Cortés later reported: "So many Indians attacked us that we could not see the ground before us. . . . Certainly we believed that to be our last day, so great was the force of the Indians and so feeble our resistance, for we were already exhausted and almost all of us were wounded and fainting from hunger."

The Spanish fought like cornered animals. The native forces were so enormous that the Spanish

The armor of King Ferdinand V (and that of his horse) on display in an Italian museum. The extension of Spain's power abroad through conquests was begun under Ferdinand. Even greater additions to the empire were made by men such as Cortés during the reign of Ferdinand's successor, Charles I.

ART RESOURCE

Aztec mask made of turquoise mosaic. Masks were often worn during religious ceremonies by priests or sacrificial victims.

would surely have been slaughtered to the last man if Cortés had not grasped an important truth about native warfare—that the armies of the Indians had no system of rank. Everyone depended on the central authority of the battle chieftain.

Cortés directed his men to concentrate all their strength on cutting down any Aztec whose elaborate armor and headdress showed him to be a leader. At last Cortés caught sight of a man in rich golden armor and high silver plumes—the Aztec commander-in-chief. Cortés was upon him at once, and in moments had him on the ground, where one of the Spanish soldiers put a spear through him. "And when the Aztec chief and many other leaders were killed," Díaz wrote, "it pleased our Lord . . . their attack slackened and all our horsemen followed them, and we felt neither hunger nor thirst."

The tide of battle had turned, and the disorganized Aztec troops fled in panic, pursued now by the Spanish. The Spaniards reveled in the butchery that followed, and Cortés became convinced that there was still a chance to recover what he had lost.

The feather headdress worn by Emperor Montezuma. Such headdresses were worn only by Aztec leaders, and they often included the long tail feathers of the sacred quetzal bird.

ART RESOURCE

The Spanish swept triumphantly back to Tlascala.

The Tlascalans remained loyal allies, and in their city Cortés reorganized his forces. He kept his men in fighting shape by leading them in vengeful raids on nearby Aztec villages, killing all the men and taking the women and children as slaves. His long-range plans never wavered. He had suffered a set-back—lost most of his men and equipment, been severely wounded, seen much of his treasure lost but he was not to be deflected from his goal. He had come to conquer Mexico, and he fully intended to do just that.

It took almost a year to prepare for the new assault. His first step was to direct the building of a navy—almost 100 miles from any body of water! It sounded fantastic to his men, but Cortés knew that the only way he could besiege the lake city of Tenochtitlán was by boat. He set his loyal, if bewildered, Indian allies to cutting timber. His carpenters sawed and planed each part, which was

A painting depicting the violent life of the conquistadors. Looting, rape, and butchery were commonplace, and Cortés's men engaged in such practices with little regard for the Christian faith they professed to believe in.

89

then numbered and packed away in a crate. In four months, Cortés had a portable fleet of 13 ships ready to be carried to Lake Texcoco, assembled, and launched against the Aztecs.

Fortune continued to favor the Spanish, although sometimes in horrible ways. One of Narváez's sailors had brought smallpox to the New World and in months an epidemic was raging through the villages and cities of the Aztecs. Unlike the Spanish, the natives had no resistance to the disease, and died by the thousands. The cities turned into graveyards as it spread through the country. The fierce Cuitláhuac, Montezuma's brother and successor, was one of the first to die. By early in the fall of 1520, the capital was so weakened that Cortés decided it was time to attack. His men terrified the natives by climbing a sacred volcano and descending into its smoking crater by rope. There, they gathered sulphur for gunpowder. A few days after Christmas, 1520, Cortés and his men set out for Tenochtitlán.

The Spanish force had grown considerably. Velásquez had sent men from Cuba to find Narváez, and the governor of Jamaica had sent men to colonize. The persuasive Cortés convinced both expeditions to join him. There were more than 500 Spanish soldiers—and some 10,000 Indians of various tribes—marching toward the capital, killing and looting and burning as they went. Cortés lifted his ban on cannibalism for the natives, and though

Indian allies of Cortés helped him to rebuild his forces and supplies for a renewed assault on Aztec strongholds.

THE AMERICAN MUSEUM OF NATURAL HISTORY

chalchicueyecā

his own troops never joined in the feasts, they did not mind feeding human flesh to the little Mexican dogs they ate. It was a healthy, almost swaggering army that established a base at Texcoco, an important city across the lake from Tenochtitlán, on December 31, 1520.

The government of Texcoco had fled, leaving the people in such confusion that they surrendered to Cortés without a fight. Many of the Texcocans joined him and fought alongside his other Indian allies.

The battle of Tenochtitlán was long and bitter. Both sides had their victories and their defeats. The new Aztec emperor, Cuauhtémoc ("Falling Eagle"), a nephew of Montezuma, was as fearless as Cuitláhuac had been, and more cunning. His military valor and his violent hatred of the Spanish had won him the election among the Aztec nobles, and he fought the invaders with the passion and decisiveness his uncle had lacked. When he succeeded in luring a troop of Spaniards into an ambush, he killed them all and sent their heads and limbs on a tour of nearby villages to prove that the Spanish were mortal. Then he tauntingly hurled them into the Spanish camp as an answer to Cortés's offers of peace.

Gradually, the Spanish advantage began to tell. Native support for Cortés grew. Tribe after tribe came to see the Spanish as liberators who could free them from Aztec domination, and Cortés's native allies finally numbered almost as many as the enemy. At its largest, the Spanish troop was nearly 900 strong, and its allies from Tlascala, Cholula, Texcoco, and other cities numbered as many as 200,000. Cortés and his tiny band of Spaniards were not toppling an empire, as has often been reported. Rather, they were exploiting a great civil war to do so.

Twelve of the 13 ships that had been transported in sections from Tlascala proved seaworthy, and Cortés's navy did its work with devastating effectiveness. Their cannon swept the lake of Aztec canoes. The aqueduct was destroyed, cutting off the city's supply of fresh water, and little by little Cortés tightened his grip on the capital. No Aztec could

The people heard a weeping woman night after night. She passed by in the middle of the night, wailing and crying out in a loud voice: "My children, we must flee far away from this city!" At other times she cried: "My children, where shall I take you?"
—from an Aztec account of omens that preceeded the arrival of the Spanish, recorded by Bernardino de Sahagún

cross his blockade with supplies. Hunger and thirst began to finish what smallpox had begun.

Whenever he could make a landing, Cortés struck swiftly and fiercely. He gave no quarter and boasted of both his treachery and his ruthlessness. He sent natives to the enemy pretending to join the Aztec side, and when they were placed in the ranks they turned their spears on the Aztecs, fighting from within. It was war to the death. Cortés reported proudly that he had personally led a mission that had found and killed 800 unarmed women and children looking for food in the streets of the city.

Cortés continued to send offers of peace and promises of respectful treatment, but Cuauhtémoc rejected them scornfully. "While one Aztec remains alive," he announced, "the war will continue." There was no choice. Tenochtitlán had to be destroyed completely.

With deliberate, systematic ferocity, Cortés and his men demolished the city, leaving no structure standing to protect the Aztecs. Building after building—house, market stall, and temple—was torched, its stone pulled into the rubble-filled street. Anyone found huddled within was killed. It is estimated that seven-eighths of this beautiful city was leveled in June and July of 1521. The surviving Indians were reduced to eating mud and drinking the brackish water of the lake. Perhaps 50,000 Aztecs starved to death during those two months in Tenochtitlán, and 250,000 were killed in battle.

Through all this slaughter, the Aztecs never deserted their faith in their god Huitzilopochtli, and fervently continued their sacrifices. The capture of a Spaniard was a special triumph, his heart a rare delicacy to the god. Only a few hundred Spanish troops fell during this bloody campaign because the Aztecs fought to take prisoners for sacrifice while the Spanish fought to kill. Twice Cortés was surrounded and almost captured, but on both occasions the determination of the Aztecs to keep him alive for their priests' obsidian knives saved him.

By August, the bodies of Aztecs littered the streets and canals of Tenochtitlán. The stench of decaying flesh was everywhere. The Aztecs knew that the war

Nothing can compare with the horrors of that siege and the agonies of the starving. We were so weakened by hunger that, little by little, the enemy forced us to retreat. Little by little they forced us to the wall.
—Aztec account of the siege of Tenochtitlán, as recorded by Bernardino de Sahagún

was over, and the survivors began trying to slip out of the city. On August 13, 1521, a Spanish patrol noticed a large canoe with the royal emblem putting out from the island of Tenochtitlán. Cortés had the vessel stopped and took Cuauhtémoc prisoner.

Not yet 25 and "very much of a gentleman, for an Indian," according to Díaz, the brave Aztec won the respect of everyone with his dignity and courage. He said that he had done "all he was bound to do to defend his own person and his people," Cortés later reported, and then "put his hand upon a dagger of mine and asked me to kill him with it."

The capture of Tenochtitlán by Cortés in August 1521. Coming after a ferocious campaign that virtually razed the city, the victory marked the end of the Aztec empire and was Cortés's greatest triumph.

Codex illustration showing Spanish cannon firing on Aztec Indians. Cortés, rightly believing that an attack by ship was the best way to besiege the lake city, had boats built and transported in sections to Lake Texcoco.

The Spaniard did not kill Cuauhtémoc—not then—but the professions of mutual respect between them did not last long. Cortés congratulated his royal captive for his valor and embraced him. Then he asked him about the gold—the great treasure of Montezuma.

Cuauhtémoc either could not or would not tell him anything. If the royal treasury—most of it left behind on *noche triste*—had been hidden by the Aztecs, its hiding place was not to be learned from him. Cortés ordered his royal captive tortured, but even scalding oil on Cuauhtémoc's feet did not loosen his tongue. The mystery of Montezuma's gold remains unsolved to this day.

Díaz called Tenochtitlán "the garden of the world," and it is said that the hardened Spanish soldiers wept at its destruction. But destroy it they did, and with its fall, and the capture of Cuauhtémoc, the Aztec empire came to an end. It had never been a true empire, administered by a central government, but was rather a loose confederation of independent tribal states under the military domination of one. Cortés's success depended far more on the loyalty he was able to inspire and the unity he was able to create among the scattered tribes of Mexico than on the military power of his own tiny band of ragged adventurers.

Now that the Aztec empire was truly in his hands, Cortés had to administer it. He had to restore order and secure his authority. He began to rebuild the city he had leveled. The captive Cuauhtémoc was restored as a puppet ruler, and instructed to order his surviving followers to work at clearing the city. Side by side with the Spanish and their Indian allies, Aztecs burned and buried the dead, hauled

A model of the Great Temple of Tenochtitlán based on existing Aztec monuments and descriptions given by Spanish conquerors. Following Cortés's victory at Tenochtitlán, a new city under Spanish administration was built and christened Mexico City.

away the rubble, and cut stone and timber for new buildings, to be erected on Spanish models. The aqueduct was repaired, the causeways reinforced, and the streets restored. Nothing of the old Tenochtitlán remained.

Many of Cortés's men thought that he should build his Spanish city elsewhere, in order to destroy its link with the barbarous Aztec past. Tenochtitlán, they argued, was an unhealthy location anyway. It was built on a swamp, and heavy stone buildings sank into the spongy ground of its marshy bed, leaning and twisting and cracking. It was more than a mile above sea level, where the air is thin and breathing is difficult. And it was constructed on islands, so it was impossible to extend without draining the lake.

But Cortés believed that there were psychological advantages in retaining the original location. He realized that, however welcome the Spanish might be as liberators, they were still outsiders, and their city would be an alien imposition on Mexico. In building a Spanish city on the very site of Tenochtitlán, placing his palace where the emperor's palace had been and the Catholic cathedral on the ruins of the great pyramid of the Aztec sun god, he made the Spanish conquest of the city a reality. Administrative power still came from the islands in Lake Texcoco, but those islands were now a European-style city, designed by a Spaniard and renamed Mexico City.

Rebuilding and reorganizing Mexico came easily to a man of Cortés's ability and determination, but establishing a legal right to his authority was another matter. He had begun this expedition on his own initiative, establishing his own settlement and dealing directly with the king of Spain. His long letters and generous tributes of gold had been aimed at winning the title and power of governor of the land he called New Spain. But he knew Velásquez was a powerful rival with as good a claim to the title as his own; Velásquez had, after all, organized and authorized the expedition, and now he was fighting Cortés with every weapon he had. It took 14 months of pleading and arguing before the king decided the

Ferdinand Magellan's *Victoria*, the first ship to circumnavigate the globe. Magellan's armada consisted of five ships when he set sail from Spain in 1519, but only the *Victoria*, with 18 survivors, completed the arduous three-year journey. Magellan himself was killed in the Philippine islands.

**Ferdinand Magellan (1480—1521), Portuguese leader of
the first expedition to circumnavigate the globe. Magellan sailed under the Spanish flag after being rebuffed in
attempts to gain military promotion in his native land.**

case, but on October 15, 1522, Charles declared Hernán Cortés of Medellín the governor of New Spain as well as captain-general and chief judge. The conqueror—whose Spanish title *conquistador* remains the one by which he is best known—had at last become a legitimate ruler of a colony.

Charles knew that great soldiers are not always great government officials, and that the very talents which made Cortés a good *conquistador* might make him a bad administrator. The king wanted to reward his loyal soldier, but he did not altogether trust him. Just to be on the safe side, he sent a royal council to supervise him. Cortés had performed astounding military feats. It now remained to be seen if he could hold on to the empire he had conquered.

Catholic cathedral built on the ruins of the great pyramid of the Aztec sun god. The building of Mexico City atop Aztec remains was a dramatic display of Spanish power. Cortés saw it as a reminder that Aztec rule had been eclipsed forever.

ART RESOURCE

**Aztec sun calendar found during a 16th-century exca-
vation of Tenochtitlán. The Aztecs followed a solar calendar of eighteen 20-day months and five "empty days."
Each of the days and months were associated with par-
ticular gods and religious symbols.**

8

The Veteran

At age 37, Cortés was at the peak of his career—but it could not last. After the conquest of Mexico, any enterprise that followed had to be something of an anticlimax. And Cortés was too young to be a retired veteran reminiscing about past triumphs.

Cortés settled down as well as he could to affairs of state. He busied himself with improving the economy of his country, and his own finances as well. He cultivated corn, cotton, and chocolate. He experimented with grapes, sugar cane, citrus, and almonds. He sent to Spain for cattle, sheep, and horses to breed. Once again he was a gentleman farmer. His life was almost the same as it had been in Cuba only a few years before.

Having besieged cities bigger than any in Europe, conducted campaigns on a heroic scale, and toppled an empire, Cortés was restless planting cane and breeding cattle. The royal representatives sent to "help" him were obviously spies sending home secret reports of his every movement. "Now that he was Governor," writes Prescott, "[he] had less real power than when he had held no legal commission at all."

UPI/BETTMANN NEWSPHOTOS

This Aztec stone figure, more than 2,000 years old, dates from the formative days of Aztec culture. The Aztec stonecutters were skilled at carving fine details into their sculptures.

An engraved portrait of Cortés. He spent years as a noble on a vast tract of land in Mexico, but continued to conduct expeditions in hopes of discovering and claiming new land for Spain.

To make matters worse, Catalina, whom Cortés had married only to make peace with Velásquez, decided to join her husband, now that he was a governor, and she brought along her large family, including her mother and sister. Cortés had had plenty of women around from the beginning of the expedition. Every chieftain had offered his daughter, and several of Montezuma's daughters were in Cortés's household, at least one of them pregnant by him. Malinche, who had ridden through everything with the *conquistador*, was still a part of his life, too. With the addition of Catalina and her huge, complaining family, life at home became intolerable.

Cortés and his quarrelsome wife argued openly, and when she died suddenly a few months later, his enemies accused him of murder. In 1523 Cortés's own restlessness, as much as his desire to consolidate the empire he had won for Spain, drew him down the coast to protect part of "his" land from the governor of Jamaica, who was trying yet again to establish a colony there.

Once Cortés was back in the saddle, he decided to prolong his vacation from Mexico City, and turned to Honduras. One of his old captains, Cristóbal de Olid—who had fought at Tlascala and Tenochtitlán—had set up his own government there, much as Cortés had done, and the *conquistador* was determined to suppress him.

The expedition to Honduras lasted from 1524 to 1526 and probably did Cortés more harm than any other he ever undertook. He was now more than 40 years old, and time was beginning to take its toll. Cortés crushed Olid and his followers and won the local Indians over to his side, but his health suffered greatly during the campaign. The venture also damaged his position.

Cortés had been careful not to leave anyone really dangerous to him behind in Mexico, and had brought the puppet ruler Cuauhtémoc and all his principal supporters. But his political enemies took advantage of his absence to spread rumors and try to influence the Spanish king against him. And during the expedition the brooding presence of the sullen Cuauhtémoc made Cortés very uncomfortable.

Broken spears lie in the roads;
we have torn our hair in
*   our grief.*
The houses are roofless now
*   and their walls*
are red with blood.
—from a poem by an anonymous Aztec survivor of the Aug. 1521 siege of Tenochtitlán

Map of Mexico showing route that Cortés followed on his various conquests. The bay of Cortés is now known as the Gulf of California.

His conscience about Tenochtitlán and the Aztecs had never been completely clear, though he had made many attempts to justify his actions in his letters to Spain. Cortés recognized that Cuauhtémoc was a symbol of Aztec independence, and that while he lived the Spanish would always be in danger. So when Cortés heard rumors of a rebellion, he had Cuauhtémoc executed.

The proud Aztec went to his death with dignity. "Now I know what it meant, Malinche, to trust to your false promises," he said. "God will demand it of you!"

Cortés's summary justice aroused considerable indignation, even among his own men. The generally admiring Díaz stated emphatically: "The ex-

Spanish explorer Francisco Coronado (1510–54) leads his band of conquistadors through what is now Kansas as he searches for the kingdom of Quivera in 1541. As Cortés's fortunes ebbed, other explorers took his place in expanding Spain's world empire.

ecution of Cuauhtémoc was most unjust; and was thought wrong by all of us."

With this execution, the royal house of the Aztecs came to an end. Cortés may have felt that it was the necessary last step in the conquest, but neither his own time nor posterity has forgiven him. Cuauhtémoc has become a hero to the Mexicans, the symbol of their national tragedy. And Cortés has become the national villain.

When Cortés returned to Mexico City, he discovered much that alarmed him. Now sick—so sick he was not recognized when he returned—he found he had been charged with tyranny, misappropriation of funds, and conspiracy to declare Mexico independent of Spain. His property had been seized and his agent executed. He was suspended from office and exiled from the city he had created.

The sentence was later lifted, and Cortés was permitted to stay in his own home, but he was not placated. On horseback, with a lance in his hand, he could take care of himself. Screaming natives with *macatls* did not frighten him. But lawyers and priests, with their coded letters and whispered reports, were more than he could take. He packed for Spain to take his case to the king in person.

Charles was not really interested in Cortés's grievances. He had concerns far more pressing than squabbles in his distant provinces. When Cortés arrived in grand style, with exotic birds and animals, Indian slaves, tubs of amber, and bales of native featherwork and embroidery, the public was fascinated, but Charles was not impressed.

Cortés had brought the king a continent and a fortune in gold, and Charles recognized it. He wanted to reward the *conquistador* for his services, but he could not really trust him as his royal representative. Viceroys and governors were selected from among the ranks of lawyers, priests, or the high nobility, not rough, ambitious soldiers, much less bold, free-spirited adventurers. Cortés had to settle for being confirmed in his title of captain-general and given a title of nobility—the first in the New World—as Marqués of the Valley of Oaxaca. With the title came a giant estate stretching from the Atlantic to the Pacific and almost one-quarter the size of Spain. It had gold and silver mines, rich plantations and productive mills. It included 22 villages and held some 23,000 Indian slaves. Cortés was probably the richest man in Mexico.

While in Spain, Cortés made a useful marriage which connected him with a rich, powerful family. Doña Juana de Zúñiga, his wife, was both attractive and intelligent, as well as rich. Better yet, she loved him and dedicated herself to his welfare. Doña Juana was to bear him six children.

If Cortés had been content with all this, he might have ended his days a happy man. But a man who has known such peaks as Cortés had scaled could not be content with the valley—even the rich, fertile Valley of Oaxaca. Although he was wealthy, honored, and happily married, Cortés felt restless.

He began to outfit new expeditions, still hoping to find the fabled riches that had drawn him to Yucatán. In 1535 the 50-year-old *conquistador* claimed Baja California for the king, but no one cared much or was particularly impressed by this uninteresting stretch of land. The expedition had cost so much money that he had had to spend his wife's dowry on it, and nothing at all was recovered.

Cortés's dreams became more grandiose and his demands more irrational. At last the cautious governor of New Spain refused to authorize any more of his expeditions.

Cortés began to brood about the injustices—real and imagined—he had suffered and was suffering, and in 1540 decided to press his case in person again. He returned to Spain almost as splendidly equipped as before and asked for an audience with the king. But he had picked a bad time. Charles was facing severe political and financial problems of his own, and his queen had recently died. The king was in no mood to listen to the problems of a disappointed old veteran. And Cortés had sent him nothing but long-winded letters of self-glorification and complaint for some time. He had become a nuisance to the court. One of his petitions, still in the royal archive, had *nay que responder* ("no need to answer") penned at the top by a minor clerk.

Cortés stayed on in Spain for six more years, growing increasingly eccentric and bitter. When he offered his advice on military matters, he was ignored or openly derided. There is a sad story—probably not true but consistent with this wretched period of the *conquistador*'s life—that he once saw the king's carriage in the street and stopped it like a man begging for alms. Charles, hoping to avoid another tedious encounter with the persistent old man, pretended not to recognize him and haughtily asked, "Who are you?"

Cortés is said to have replied, "I am a man, Sire, who has brought you more provinces than your father and grandfather bequeathed you cities."

Cervantes (Miguel de Cervantes Saavedra) (1547–1616), famed Spanish writer and the author of *Don Quixote*, was born the year that Cortés died.

Spanish explorer Francisco Pizarro (1475–1541), with
King Charles in the 1520s. Pizarro conquered the Incan
empire of South America in 1533.

HISTORIA
DE NUEVA-ESPAÑA,
ESCRITA POR SU ESCLARECIDO CONQUISTADOR
HERNAN CORTES,
AUMENTADA
CON OTROS DOCUMENTOS, Y NOTAS,
POR EL ILUSTRISSIMO SEÑOR
DON FRANCISCO ANTONIO
LORENZANA,
ARZOBISPO DE MEXICO.

OPIBUS CLARA, RELIGIONE NOBILIOR.

CON LAS LICENCIAS NECESARIAS
En México en la Imprenta del Superior Gobierno, del Br. D. Joseph Antonio de Hogal
en la Calle de Tiburcio. Año de 1770.

Frontispiece from a book, published in 1770, called *Historia de Nueva-España* (The History of New Spain). The book consisted of five letters that Cortés wrote to King Charles during the course of his Mexican conquests. The letters are the only samples of Cortés's writing known to exist.

Cortés eventually realized he was wasting his time. He decided to go home. He was 62 now, and knew he did not have much time left. In fact, he had even less than he thought, and he never reached Mexico. On December 2, 1547, while preparing to return to Oaxaca, the old *conquistador* died.

Cortés's death excited little comment. New heroes had come, new lands had been discovered and conquered, and Cortés had become a part of history.

Where the first and greatest of the *conquistadors* belongs in history is a question that can never be fully answered. No one can deny his cruelty, and perhaps it is not surprising that no statue or plaque commemorates him in the country that he created. Yet if he destroyed an old and highly developed civilization, he also gave the country much. He brought it a common language in place of a hundred Indian tongues. He introduced a religion which even the Indians came to accept as an improvement on the cruel and bloody beliefs it replaced. Finally, he brought it unity. Mexico had been ready to fly apart for a century and had suffered from oppressors far worse than the Spanish. Most of the natives of Mexico saw Cortés and his men as liberators.

The Europeans exploited the Indians for 300 years, giving them little and using them like livestock; but they did not cage them to be fattened for ritual slaughter like the Aztecs. Mexico has known much internal dissension, but it is a nation and not a conglomeration of terrified tribes paying tribute

Cortés presenting the "New World" to the Spanish King Charles I. Even though the new territories Cortés had secured for Spain proved immensely valuable to the growing empire, Cortés himself ultimately fell out of favor with the sovereign.

Aztec warrior chief in full regalia. The dress of the Aztec nobles was governed by a strict code that stated what ornaments could be worn by officials of different ranks.

in sacrificial victims to an insatiable war god. For this, Hernán Cortés must receive a large share of the credit.

Cortés was undoubtedly greedy. He not only stripped the country of every ounce of gold he could find, he took more than his own share whenever he could get away with it. But he was more than a vulgar money-grubber.

When the Spanish first met the Aztecs, in 1519, they told Montezuma's bewildered ambassadors that they wanted gold. "We Spanish suffer from a disease of the heart," Cortés improvised, "which can be cured only by gold." His glib explanation was truer than he realized, and the disease was to prove fatal to many of his countrymen. Cortés, however, survived his case of that disease because, greedy and brutal though he was, he was ultimately prompted by higher motives and a greater vision than gold. His unflinching courage and shrewd perception were at the service not merely of a desire for wealth, or fame, or power. He was spurred on by a genuine dedication to his God and his king.

Why did Cortés not collect a few souvenirs and hurry back from Yucatán, like Fernández de Córdoba and Grijalva? Or stay and provide a rare meal for cannibals, like the hapless Valdivia? Partly, of course, because he was braver and smarter and luckier than they were. But in very large measure, Hernán Cortés placed his stamp on history because he was governed by a great principle, greater than gold, greater than glory. His devotion to this principle cost him dearly, but ultimately civilization is the richer for it.

A conquistador as drawn by American artist Frederic Remington (1861–1909). Though some historians say Cortés was nothing more than a greedy and brutal soldier, others believe he should be remembered for his courage and great leadership qualities.

Frederic Remington

Further Reading

Cortés, Hernando. *Letters from Mexico*. New York: Grossman Publishers, 1944.

de Madariaga, Salvador. *Hernán Cortés: Conqueror of Mexico*. Coral Gables, Fla.: University of Miami Press, 1962.

de Sahagún, Bernardino. *The War of Conquest: How it was Waged Here in Mexico*. Salt Lake City: University of Utah Press, 1978.

Díaz del Castillo, Bernal. *The Discovery and Conquest of Mexico, 1517–1521*. New York: Farrar, Straus & Cudahy, 1956.

Innes, Hammond. *The Conquistadors*. New York: Alfred A. Knopf, 1969.

Johnson, William Weber. *Cortés*. Boston: Little, Brown, & Co., 1975.

León-Portilla, Miguel. *The Broken Spears: The Aztec Account of the Conquest of Mexico*. Boston: Beacon Press, 1962.

López de Gómara, Francisco. *Cortés: The Life of the Conqueror, by his Secretary*. Berkeley: University of California Press, 1964.

Vaillant, George C. *Aztecs of Mexico*. Garden City, N.J.: Doubleday, 1953.

von Hagen, Victor W. *The Ancient Sun Kingdoms of the Americas*. Cleveland: World Publishing Co., 1961.

White, Jon Manchip. *Cortés and the Downfall of the Aztec Empire*. New York: St. Martin's Press, 1971.

Chronology

1485	Hernán Cortés born in Medellín, Spain
1499–1501	Studies law and Latin at the University of Salamanca
1504	Goes to Hispaniola (now the Dominican Republic)
1511	Acts as secretary to Diego Velásquez on expedition to Cuba
Feb. 1519	Leads expedition to Yucatán, Mexico
April 1519	Founds city of Veracruz; destroys ships to prevent return of expedition
Sept. 1519	Defeats the Tlascalan Indians
Oct. 1519	Cholula massacre
Nov. 1519	Cortés arrives at Aztec capital, Tenochtitlán (now Mexico City)
April 1520	Tenochtitlán massacre
June 30, 1520	Retreat from Tenochtitlán, *la noche triste*
July 1520	Defeats the Aztecs at Otumba
May–Aug. 1521	Siege of Tenochtitlán
Aug. 13, 1521	Fall of the Aztec empire
1522	Cortés named governor of New Spain
1524–26	Leads expedition to Honduras
1526	Suspended from office after being charged with misconduct
1528	Returns to Spain to plead his cause Named Marqués of the Valley of Oaxaca
1530	Returns to Mexico
1540	Visits Spain to protest lack of authority
Dec. 2, 1547	Dies near Seville, Spain

Index

Dennis Wepman has a graduate degree in linguistics from Columbia University and has written widely on sociology, linguistics, popular culture, and American folklore. He now teaches English at Queens College of the City University of New York. He is the author of *Simón Bolívar*, *Jomo Kenyatta*, *Alexander the Great*, *Benito Juárez*, and *Adolf Hitler* in the Chelsea House series WORLD LEADERS PAST & PRESENT.

Arthur M. Schlesinger, jr., taught history at Harvard for many years and is currently Albert Schweitzer Professor of the Humanities at City University of New York. He is the author of numerous highly praised works in American history and has twice been awarded the Pulitzer Prize. He served in the White House as special assistant to Presidents Kennedy and Johnson.